chicken

100 everyday recipes

This edition published in 2013
LOVE FOOD is an imprint of Parragon Books Ltd

Parragon
Chartist House
15–17 Trim Street
Bath, BA1 1HA, UK

ISBN: 978-1-4723-2505-1

Printed in China

Produced by Ivy Contract
Photography by Charlie Paul

Notes for the Reader

This book uses imperial, metric, or US cup measurements. Follow the same units of measurement through-out; do not mix imperial and metric. All spoon measurements are level: teaspoons are assumed to be 5 ml, and tablespoons are assumed to be 15 ml. Unless otherwise stated, milk is assumed to be full fat, eggs and individual vegetables are medium, and pepper is freshly ground black pepper.

The times given are an approximate guide only. Preparation times differ according to the techniques used by different people and the cooking times may also vary from those given. Optional ingredients, variations or serving suggestions have not been included in the calculations.

Recipes using raw or very lightly cooked eggs should be avoided by infants, the elderly, pregnant women, convalescents, and anyone suffering from an illness. Pregnant and breastfeeding women are advised to avoid eating peanuts and peanut products. Sufferers from nut allergies should be aware that some of the ready-made ingredients used in the recipes in this book may contain nuts. Always check the packaging before use. Vegetarians should be aware that some of the ready-made ingredients used in the recipes in this book may contain animal products. Always check the packaging before use.

chicken

introduction

Chicken has become one of the most useful and popular meats in nearly all cultures around the world. The reasons for this are many, not least that chickens are relatively quick and easy to raise, and do not require acres of lush grassland! It is worth bearing in mind that a free-range, corn-fed chicken might cost a little more, but it will have a far superior flavor to one that has been intensively farmed.

From a nutritional point of view, chicken is an excellent source of protein, B vitamins, and minerals such as zinc and iron. It is naturally low in fat and has no carbohydrates, making it the dream food for those who need to keep their weight or cholesterol levels in check. It is very quick and easy to cook, too, so there need be no excuses about not having enough time to produce a healthy, well-balanced meal!

And from a gastronomic point of view? There are so many options that you could serve chicken every day of the week and still not run out of ideas! Chicken can be cooked very simply—roasted, chargrilled, broiled, stir-fried, or pan-fried—and served with potatoes or rice and salad greens or lightly cooked vegetables. And when you have a little more time to spare, the choices are endless. If you like rice, you can go for a creamy Italian risotto or a saffron-colored Spanish paella; and if you are a pasta lover, you will find some fantastic sauces. If Mexican food is your thing, there are traditional recipes to suit you; and there are Chinese, Thai, and Indian dishes to satisfy any spice cravings.

Whatever your choice, you will enjoy the flavor and variety these recipes have to offer.

soups, starters & salads

cream of chicken soup

ingredients

serves 4

3 tbsp butter

4 shallots, chopped

1 leek, sliced

1 lb/450 g skinless, boneless chicken breasts, chopped

1³⁄₄ pints/1 litre/2½ cups chicken stock

1 tbsp chopped fresh parsley

1 tbsp chopped fresh thyme, plus extra sprigs to garnish

³⁄₄ cup heavy cream

salt and pepper

method

1 Melt the butter in a saucepan over medium heat. Add the shallots and cook, stirring, for 3 minutes, until softened. Add the leek and cook for another 5 minutes, stirring. Add the chicken, stock, parsley, and thyme and season. Bring to a boil, then simmer for 25 minutes, until the chicken is cooked through. Remove from the heat and let stand to cool for 10 minutes.

2 Transfer the soup to a food processor or blender and process until smooth (you may need to do this in batches). Return the soup to the rinsed-out pan and warm over low heat for 5 minutes.

3 Stir in the cream and cook for another 2 minutes, then remove from the heat and ladle into serving bowls. Garnish with sprigs of thyme and serve immediately.

variation

For a low fat option, omit the heavy cream and replace half the chicken stock with low fat milk. The soup will still taste smooth and creamy.

chicken & potato soup with bacon

ingredients

serves 4

1 tbsp butter
2 garlic cloves, chopped
1 onion, sliced
9 oz/250 g smoked, lean
    bacon, chopped
2 large leeks, sliced
2 tbsp all-purpose flour
1¾ pints/1 litre/4 cups
    chicken stock
1 lb 12 oz/800 g potatoes,
    chopped
7 oz/200 g skinless, boneless
    chicken breast, chopped
4 tbsp heavy cream
salt and pepper
broiled strips of bacon and sprigs
    of fresh flat-leaf parsley,
    to garnish

method

1 Melt the butter in a large saucepan over medium heat. Add the garlic and onion and cook, stirring, for 3 minutes, until slightly softened. Add the chopped bacon and leeks and cook for another 3 minutes, stirring continuously.

2 In a bowl, mix the flour with enough stock to make a smooth paste, then stir it into the pan. Cook, stirring, for 2 minutes. Pour in the remaining stock, then add the potatoes and chicken. Season with salt and pepper. Bring to a boil, then lower the heat and simmer for 25 minutes, until the chicken and potatoes are tender and cooked through.

3 Stir in the cream and cook for another 2 minutes, then remove from the heat and ladle into serving bowls. Garnish with the broiled bacon and flat-leaf parsley, and serve immediately.

chicken & broccoli soup

ingredients

serves 4–6

8 oz/225 g head broccoli

2 oz/55 g unsalted butter

1 onion, chopped

8 oz/225 g/1⅓ cups basmati rice

8 oz/225 g skinless, boneless
chicken breast, cut into
thin slivers

1 oz/25 g/scant ¼ cup all-purpose
whole wheat flour

10 fl oz/300 ml/1¼ cups milk

16 fl oz/500 ml/2 cups chicken
stock

2 oz/55 g/generous ⅓ cup corn
kernels

salt and pepper

method

1 Break the broccoli into small florets and cook in a pan
of lightly salted boiling water for 3 minutes, drain, then
plunge into cold water and set aside.

2 Melt the butter in a pan over medium heat, add the
onion, rice, and chicken, and cook for 5 minutes,
stirring frequently.

3 Remove the pan from the heat and stir in the flour.
Return to the heat and cook for 2 minutes, stirring
constantly. Stir in the milk and then the stock. Bring to
a boil, stirring continuously, then reduce the heat and
let simmer for 10 minutes.

4 Drain the broccoli and add to the pan with the corn
and salt and pepper. Let simmer for 5 minutes, or until
the rice is tender, then serve.

thai chicken-coconut soup

ingredients

serves 4

4 oz/115 g dried vermicelli noodles
2 pints/1.2 litres/5 cups chicken
    or vegetable stock
1 lemongrass stalk, crushed
½-inch/1-cm piece fresh ginger,
    peeled and finely chopped
2 fresh kaffir lime leaves, thinly
    sliced
1 fresh red chile, or to taste,
    seeded and thinly sliced
2 skinless, boneless chicken
    breasts, thinly sliced
scant 1 cup coconut cream
2–3 tbsp Thai fish sauce
1–2 tbsp fresh lime juice
⅔ cup beansprouts
4 scallions, green part only,
    finely sliced
fresh cilantro leaves, to garnish

method

1 Soak the dried noodles in a large bowl with enough lukewarm water to cover for 20 minutes, until soft. Or, cook according to the package directions. Drain well and set aside.

2 Meanwhile, bring the stock to a boil in a large pan over high heat. Lower the heat, add the lemongrass, ginger, lime leaves, and chile, and cook for 5 minutes. Add the chicken and continue simmering for another 3 minutes, or until cooked.

3 Stir in the coconut cream, fish sauce, and 1 tablespoon of lime juice and continue simmering for 3 minutes. Add the beansprouts and scallions and simmer for another 1 minute.

4 Taste and gradually add extra fish sauce or lime juice to the pan, if needed. Remove and discard the lemongrass stalk.

5 Divide the vermicelli noodles among 4 bowls. Bring the soup back to a boil, then add to each bowl. The heat of the soup will warm the noodles. To garnish, sprinkle with cilantro leaves.

chicken & tarragon soup

ingredients

serves 4

2 oz/55 g unsalted butter
1 large onion, chopped
10½ oz/300 g cooked skinless
   chicken, finely shredded
20 fl oz/625 ml/2½ cups
   chicken stock
1 tbsp chopped fresh tarragon
5 fl oz/150 ml/⅔ cup heavy cream
salt and pepper
fresh tarragon leaves, to garnish
deep-fried croutons, to serve

method

1 Melt the butter in a large pan and fry the onion for 3 minutes.

2 Add the chicken to the pan with half of the chicken stock. Bring to a boil, then reduce the heat and let simmer for 20 minutes. Let cool, then process until smooth in a blender or food processor.

3 Return the soup to the pan to heat through. Add the remainder of the stock, season with salt and pepper, and heat through. Add the chopped tarragon, then transfer the soup to individual serving bowls and stir in the cream.

4 Garnish the soup with fresh tarragon and serve with deep-fried croutons.

clear soup with mushrooms & chicken

ingredients

serves 4

1 oz/25 g/¼ cup dried porcini
   or other mushrooms
32 fl oz/1 liter/4 cups water
2 tbsp vegetable or peanut oil
4 oz/115 g mushrooms, sliced
2 garlic cloves, coarsely chopped
2-inch/5-cm piece fresh galangal,
   thinly sliced
2 chicken breast portions
   (on the bone, skin on)
8 oz/225 g baby cremini or white
   mushrooms, cut into fourths
juice of ½ lime
sprigs fresh flat-leaf parsley,
   to garnish

method

1 Place the dried mushrooms in a small bowl and pour over hot water to cover. Set aside to soak for 20–30 minutes. Drain the mushrooms, reserving the soaking liquid. Cut off the stalks and chop the caps coarsely.

2 Pour the reserved soaking water into a pan with the water and bring to a boil. Reduce the heat to a simmer.

3 Meanwhile, heat the oil in a wok and stir-fry the soaked mushrooms, sliced fresh mushrooms, garlic, and galangal for 3–4 minutes. Add to the pan of hot water with the chicken breasts. Let simmer for 10–15 minutes, until the meat comes off the bones easily.

4 Remove the chicken from the pan. Peel off and set aside the skin. Remove the meat from the bones, slice, and set aside. Return the skin and bones to the stock and let simmer for an additional 30 minutes.

5 Remove the pan from the heat and strain the stock into a clean pan through a strainer lined with cheesecloth. Bring back to a boil and add the cremini or white mushrooms, sliced chicken, and lime juice. Reduce the heat and let simmer for 8-10 minutes. Ladle into warmed bowls, garnish with parsley sprigs, and serve immediately.

chicken crostini

ingredients

serves 4

12 slices French bread
    or country bread
4 tbsp olive oil
2 garlic cloves, chopped
2 tbsp finely chopped fresh
    oregano
3½ oz/100 g cold roast chicken,
    cut into small, thin slices
4 tomatoes, sliced
12 thin slices of goat cheese
12 black olives, pitted and chopped
salt and pepper
fresh salad greens, to serve

method

1 Put the bread under a preheated medium broiler and lightly toast on both sides. Meanwhile, pour the olive oil into a bowl and add the garlic and oregano. Season with salt and pepper and mix well. Remove the toasted bread slices from the broiler and brush them on one side only with the oil mixture.

2 Place the bread slices, oiled sides up, on a cookie sheet. Put some sliced chicken on top of each one, followed by a slice of tomato.

3 Divide the slices of goat cheese among the bread slices, then top with the chopped olives. Drizzle over the remaining oil mixture and transfer to a preheated oven, 350°F/180°C. Bake for about 5 minutes, or until the cheese is golden and starting to melt.

4 Remove from the oven and serve on a bed of fresh salad greens.

chicken-noodle soup

ingredients

serves 4–6

2 skinless, boneless chicken breasts

3½ pints/2 liters/8 cups water

1 onion, with skin left on,
    cut in half

1 large garlic clove, cut in half

½-inch/1-cm piece fresh ginger,
    peeled and sliced

4 black peppercorns, lightly
    crushed

4 cloves

2 star anise

1 carrot, peeled

1 celery stalk, chopped

3½ oz/100 g baby corn, cut in half
    lengthwise and chopped

2 scallions, finely shredded

4 oz/115 g dried rice vermicelli
    noodles

salt and pepper

method

1 Put the chicken breasts and water in a pan over high heat and bring to a boil. Lower the heat to its lowest setting and let simmer, skimming the surface until no more foam rises. Add the onion, garlic, ginger, peppercorns, cloves, star anise, and a pinch of salt and continue to simmer for 20 minutes, or until the chicken is tender and cooked through. Meanwhile, grate the carrot along its length on the coarse side of a grater so you get long, thin strips.

2 Strain the chicken, reserving about 2 pints/1.25 liters/ 5 cups stock, but discarding any flavoring ingredients. (At this point you can let the stock cool and refrigerate overnight, so any fat solidifies and can be lifted off and discarded.) Return the stock to the rinsed-out pan with the carrot, celery, baby corn, and scallions and bring to a boil. Boil until the baby corn are almost tender, then add the noodles and continue boiling for 2 minutes.

3 Meanwhile, chop the chicken, add it to the pan, and continue cooking for about 1 minute until the chicken is reheated and the noodles are soft. Add seasoning and serve in warmed bowls.

crispy chicken & ham croquettes

ingredients

makes 8

4 tbsp olive oil

4 tbsp all-purpose flour

7 fl oz/200 ml/scant 1 cup milk

4 oz/115 g cooked chicken, ground

2 oz/55 g serrano or cooked ham,
    very finely chopped

1 tbsp chopped fresh flat-leaf
    parsley, plus extra sprigs
    to garnish

small pinch of freshly
    grated nutmeg

1 egg, beaten

2 oz/55 g/1 cup day-old white
    bread crumbs

corn oil, for deep-frying

salt and pepper

garlic mayonnaise, to serve

method

1 Heat the olive oil in a pan. Stir in the flour to form a paste and cook gently for 1 minute, stirring constantly. Gradually stir in the milk until smooth and slowly bring to a boil, stirring, until the mixture boils and thickens.

2 Remove from the heat, add the ground chicken, and beat until the mixture is smooth. Add the chopped ham, parsley, and nutmeg and mix well together. Season with salt and pepper. Put in a dish and let stand for 30 minutes, until cool, then cover and let rest in the refrigerator for 2–3 hours or overnight.

3 Pour the beaten egg onto a plate and spread out the bread crumbs on another plate. Divide the chilled chicken mixture into 8 portions, then shape to form cylindrical croquettes. Dip them, one at a time, in the beaten egg, then roll in the bread crumbs to coat. Let chill in the refrigerator for 1 hour.

4 Heat the oil in a deep-fryer to 350–375°F/180–190°C. Add the croquettes, in batches to prevent the temperature of the oil dropping, and deep-fry for 5–10 minutes, or until golden brown and crispy. Remove with a slotted spoon and drain well on paper towels.

5 Serve the croquettes piping hot, garnished with parsley sprigs, with garlic mayonnaise.

chicken in lemon & garlic

ingredients

serves 6–8

4 large skinless, boneless
    chicken breasts
5 tbsp Spanish olive oil
1 onion, finely chopped
6 garlic cloves,
    finely chopped
grated rind of 1 lemon, finely pared
    zest of 1 lemon and juice of
    both lemons
4 tbsp chopped fresh flat-leaf
    parsley, plus extra to garnish
salt and pepper
lemon wedges and crusty bread,
    to serve

method

1 Using a sharp knife, slice the chicken breasts widthwise into very thin slices. Heat the olive oil in a large, heavy-bottom skillet, add the onion and cook for 5 minutes, or until softened, but not browned. Add the garlic and cook for an additional 30 seconds.

2 Add the sliced chicken to the skillet and cook gently for 5–10 minutes, stirring from time to time, until all the ingredients are lightly browned and the chicken is tender.

3 Add the grated lemon rind and the lemon juice and let it bubble. At the same time, deglaze the skillet by scraping and stirring all the bits on the bottom of the skillet into the juices with a wooden spoon. Remove the skillet from the heat, stir in the parsley, and season with salt and pepper.

4 Transfer, piping hot, to a warmed serving dish. Sprinkle with the pared lemon zest, garnish with the parsley, and serve with lemon wedges for squeezing over the chicken, accompanied by chunks or slices of crusty bread for mopping up the juices.

soy chicken wings

ingredients

serves 3–4

9 oz/250 g chicken wings,
    defrosted if frozen
8 fl oz/250 ml/1 cup water
1 tbsp sliced scallion
1-inch/2.5-cm piece of fresh
    ginger, cut into 4 slices
2 tbsp light soy sauce
½ tsp dark soy sauce
1 star anise
1 tsp sugar

method

1 Wash and dry the chicken wings. In a small pan, bring the water to a boil, then add the chicken, scallion, and fresh ginger and bring back to a boil.

2 Add the remaining ingredients, then cover and simmer for 30 minutes.

3 Using a slotted spoon, remove the chicken wings from any remaining liquid and serve hot.

chicken liver pâté

ingredients

serves 6–8

6 oz/175 g unsalted butter
1 lb 2 oz/500 g chicken livers,
    thawed if frozen, and trimmed
½ tbsp sunflower oil
2 shallots, finely chopped
2 large garlic cloves, finely
    chopped
2½ tbsp Madeira or brandy
2 tbsp heavy cream
1 tsp dried thyme
¼ tsp ground allspice
salt and pepper
toasted slices brioche and
    mixed salad greens,
    to serve

method

1 Melt 1 oz/30 g of the butter in a large skillet over medium-high heat. Add the chicken livers and stir for 5 minutes, or until they are brown on the outside, but still slightly pink in the centers. Work in batches, if necessary, to avoid overcrowding the pan.

2 Transfer the livers and their cooking juices to a food processor. Melt another 1 oz/30 g of the butter with the oil in the pan. Add the shallots and garlic and sauté, stirring frequently, for 2–3 minutes, until the shallots are soft, but not brown.

3 Add the Madeira and scrape up any cooking juices from the base. Stir in the cream, then the thyme, allspice, salt, and pepper. Pour this mixture, with the cooking juices, into the food processor with the livers. Add the remaining butter, cut into small pieces.

4 Whiz the mixture in the food processor until smooth. Taste, and adjust the seasoning if necessary. Let the mixture cool slightly, then scrape into a serving bowl and set aside to allow the pâté to cool completely.

5 Serve immediately, or cover the pâté and store in the refrigerator for up to 3 days and let stand at room temperature for 30 minutes before serving. Serve with hot toasted brioche and mixed salad greens.

mixed greens with warm chicken livers

ingredients

serves 4

9 oz/250 g mixed salad greens,
    torn into bite-size pieces
2 tbsp chopped fresh
    flat-leaf parsley
2 tbsp snipped fresh chives
3–4 tbsp olive oil
3½ oz/100 g shallots,
    finely chopped
1 large garlic clove,
    finely chopped
1 lb 2 oz/500 g chicken livers,
    cored, trimmed and halved
3 tbsp raspberry vinegar
salt and pepper
French bread, to serve (optional)

method

1 Toss the salad greens with the parsley and chives and divide among individual plates.

2 Heat 2 tablespoons of the oil in a sauté pan or skillet over medium–high heat. Add the shallots and garlic and sauté for 2 minutes, or until the shallots are soft, but not brown.

3 Add an extra tablespoon of the oil to the sauté pan and heat. Add the chicken livers and sauté for 5 minutes, or until they appear just pink in the center when cut in half. Add a little extra oil to the pan while the chicken livers are sautéeing, if necessary.

4 Increase the heat to high, then add the raspberry vinegar and stir quickly. Season with salt and pepper, then spoon the livers and cooking juices over the mixed greens. Serve immediately with French bread, if using.

chicken, cheese & arugula salad

ingredients

serves 4

5½ oz/150 g arugula leaves
2 celery stalks, trimmed and sliced
½ cucumber, sliced
2 scallions, trimmed and sliced
2 tbsp chopped fresh parsley
1 oz/25 g walnut pieces
12 oz/350 g boneless roast
    chicken, sliced
4½ oz/125 g Stilton cheese, cubed
handful of seedless red grapes,
    cut in half (optional)
salt and pepper

dressing
2 tbsp olive oil
1 tbsp sherry vinegar
1 tsp Dijon mustard
1 tbsp chopped mixed herbs

method

1 Wash the arugula leaves, pat dry with paper towels, and put them into a large salad bowl. Add the celery, cucumber, scallions, parsley, and walnuts and mix together well. Transfer onto a large serving platter. Arrange the chicken slices over the salad, then scatter over the cheese. Add the red grapes, if using. Season well with salt and pepper.

2 To make the dressing, put all the ingredients into a screw-top jar and shake well. Alternatively, put them into a bowl and mix together well. Drizzle the dressing over the salad and serve.

roast chicken salad with orange dressing

ingredients

serves 4

9 oz/250 g young spinach leaves
handful of fresh parsley leaves
½ cucumber, thinly sliced
3¼ oz/90 g/generous ¾ cup
   walnuts, toasted and chopped
12 oz/350 g boneless lean roast
   chicken, thinly sliced
2 red apples
1 tbsp lemon juice
fresh flat-leaf parsley sprigs,
   to garnish
orange wedges, to serve

orange dressing

2 tbsp extra virgin olive oil
juice of 1 orange
finely grated rind of ½ orange
1 tbsp sour cream

method

1 Wash and drain the spinach and parsley leaves, if necessary, then arrange on a large serving platter. Top with the cucumber and walnuts. Arrange the chicken slices on top of the leaves.

2 Core the apples, then cut them in half. Cut each half into slices and brush with the lemon juice to prevent discoloration. Arrange the apple slices over the salad.

3 Place all the dressing ingredients in a screw-top jar, screw on the lid tightly, and shake well until thoroughly combined. Drizzle the dressing over the salad, garnish with parsley sprigs, and serve immediately with orange wedges.

chicken pinwheels with blue cheese & herbs

ingredients

serves 4

2 tbsp pine nuts, lightly toasted
2 tbsp chopped fresh parsley
2 tbsp chopped fresh thyme
1 garlic clove, chopped
1 tbsp grated lemon rind
4 large, skinless, boneless chicken breasts
9 oz/250 g blue cheese, such as Stilton, crumbled
salt and pepper
twists of lemon and sprigs of fresh parsley, to garnish
fresh salad greens, to serve

method

1 Put the pine nuts into a food processor with the parsley, thyme, garlic, and lemon rind. Season with salt and pepper.

2 Pound the chicken breasts lightly to flatten them. Spread them on one side with the pine nut mixture, then top with the cheese. Roll them up from one short end to the other, so that the filling is enclosed. Wrap the rolls individually in aluminum foil, and seal well. Transfer to a steamer, or a metal colander placed over a pan of boiling water, cover tightly, and steam for 10–12 minutes, or until cooked through.

3 Arrange the salad greens on a large serving platter. Remove the chicken from the heat, discard the foil, and cut the chicken rolls into slices. Arrange the slices over the salad greens, garnish with twists of lemon, and sprigs of parsley, and serve.

cajun chicken salad

ingredients

serves 4

4 skinless, boneless chicken
   breasts, about 5 oz/140 g each
4 tsp Cajun seasoning
2 tsp corn oil (optional)
1 ripe mango, peeled, pitted, and
   cut into thick slices
7 oz/200 g mixed salad greens
1 red onion, thinly sliced and
   cut in half
6 oz/175 g cooked beet, diced
3 oz/85 g radishes, sliced
2 oz/55 g/scant ½ cup walnut
   halves
4 tbsp walnut oil
1–2 tsp Dijon mustard
1 tbsp lemon juice
2 tbsp sesame seeds
salt and pepper

method

1 Make 3 diagonal slashes across each chicken breast. Put the chicken into a shallow dish and sprinkle all over with the Cajun seasoning. Cover and let chill for at least 30 minutes.

2 When ready to cook, brush a grill pan with the corn oil, if using. Heat over high heat until very hot and a few drops of water sprinkled into the pan sizzle immediately. Add the chicken and cook for 7–8 minutes on each side, or until thoroughly cooked. If still slightly pink in the center, cook a little longer. Remove the chicken and set aside.

3 Add the mango slices to the pan and cook for 2 minutes on each side. Remove from the pan and set aside.

4 Meanwhile, arrange the salad greens in a salad bowl, reserving a few for a garnish, and sprinkle over the onion, beet, radishes, and walnut halves.

5 Put the walnut oil, mustard, lemon juice, salt, and pepper in a screw-top jar and shake until well blended. Pour over the salad and sprinkle with the sesame seeds.

6 Arrange the mango and the salad on a serving plate, top with the chicken breast and garnish with a few of the salad greens.

gingered chicken & vegetable salad

ingredients

serves 4

4 skinless, boneless chicken breasts
4 scallions, chopped
1-inch/2.5-cm piece fresh ginger, finely chopped
2 garlic cloves, crushed
2 tbsp vegetable or peanut oil

salad

1 tbsp vegetable or peanut oil
1 onion, sliced
2 garlic cloves, chopped
4 oz/115 g baby corn, halved
4 oz/115 g snow peas, halved lengthwise
1 red bell pepper, seeded and sliced
3-inch/7.5-cm piece cucumber, peeled, seeded, and sliced
4 tbsp Thai soy sauce
1 tbsp jaggery or soft light brown sugar
few Thai basil leaves
6 oz/175 g fine egg noodles

method

1 Cut the chicken into large cubes, each about 1 inch. Mix the scallions, ginger, garlic, and oil together in a shallow dish and add the chicken. Cover and let marinate for at least 3 hours. Lift the meat out of the marinade and set aside.

2 To make the salad, heat the oil in a wok or large skillet and cook the onion for 1–2 minutes before adding the rest of the vegetables, except the cucumber. Cook for 2–3 minutes, until just tender. Add the cucumber, half the soy sauce, the sugar, and the basil, and mix gently.

3 Meanwhile, soak the noodles for 2–3 minutes (check the package instructions) or until tender, and drain well. Sprinkle the remaining soy sauce over them and arrange on plates. Top with the cooked vegetables.

4 Add a little more oil to the wok, if necessary, and cook the chicken over fairly high heat until browned on all sides. Arrange the chicken cubes on top of the salad and serve hot or warm.

red chicken salad

ingredients

serves 4

4 boneless chicken breasts

2 tbsp red curry paste

2 tbsp vegetable or peanut oil

1 head Napa cabbage, shredded

6 oz/175 g bok choy, torn into
    large pieces

½ savoy cabbage, shredded

2 shallots, finely chopped

2 garlic cloves, crushed

1 tbsp rice wine vinegar

2 tbsp sweet chili sauce

2 tbsp Thai soy sauce

method

1 Slash the flesh of the chicken several times and rub the curry paste into each cut. Cover and let chill overnight.

2 Cook in a heavy-bottom pan over medium heat or on a grill pan for 5–6 minutes, turning once or twice, until cooked through. Keep warm.

3 Heat 1 tablespoon of the oil in a wok or large skillet and stir-fry the Napa cabbage, bok choy, and savoy cabbage until just wilted. Add the remaining oil, shallots, and garlic, and stir-fry until just tender, but not browned. Add the vinegar, chili sauce, and soy. Remove from the heat.

4 Arrange the leaves on 4 serving plates. Slice the chicken, arrange on the greens, and drizzle the hot dressing over. Serve immediately.

thai chicken salad

ingredients

serves 6

vegetable oil spray
4 oz/115g skinless chicken breast,
    cut lengthwise horizontally
3 limes

dressing

1 tbsp finely shredded lemongrass
1 small green chile, finely chopped
3 tbsp lime juice
½-inch/1-cm fresh ginger, peeled
    and thinly sliced into strips
1½ tsp sugar
2 tbsp white wine vinegar
3 fl oz/90 ml/⅓ cup water
1½ tsp cornstarch

salad

1 oz/25 g rice vermicelli noodles
1¾ oz/50 g bell peppers, seeded
1¾ oz/50 g carrot
1¾ oz/50 g zucchini
1¾ oz/50 g snow peas
1¾ oz/50 g baby corn
1¾ oz/50 g broccoli florets
1¾ oz/50 g bok choy
4 tbsp roughly chopped fresh
    cilantro leaves

method

1 To make the dressing, put all the dressing ingredients, except the cornstarch, into a small pan over low heat and bring to a boil. Blend the cornstarch with a little cold water, gradually add to the pan, stirring continuously, and cook until thickened. Remove from the heat and let cool.

2 Heat a grill pan over high heat and spray lightly with oil. Add the chicken and cook for 2 minutes on each side, or until thoroughly cooked through. Remove the chicken from the pan and shred.

3 To make the salad, cover the rice vermicelli with boiling water then let it cool in the water. Meanwhile, finely slice the bell peppers, carrot, zucchini, snow peas, and baby corn into strips. Cut the broccoli florets into ¼-inch/5-mm pieces and shred the bok choy. Drain the rice vermicelli and put all the salad ingredients with the chicken into a large bowl. Pour over the dressing and toss together, making sure that all the ingredients are well coated.

4 Cover and refrigerate for at least 2 hours before serving. Serve with the juice from half a lime squeezed over each portion.

lunch & light meals

spicy tomato chicken

ingredients

serves 4

1 lb 2 oz/500 g skinless, boneless
    chicken breasts
3 tbsp tomato paste
2 tbsp honey
2 tbsp Worcestershire sauce
1 tbsp chopped fresh rosemary
9 oz/250 g cherry tomatoes
fresh rosemary sprigs, to garnish
freshly cooked couscous or rice,
    to serve

method

1 Using a sharp knife, cut the chicken into 1-inch/2.5-cm chunks and place in a bowl. Mix the tomato paste, honey, Worcestershire sauce, and rosemary together in a separate bowl, then add to the chicken, stirring to coat evenly.

2 Soak 8 wooden skewers in a bowl of cold water for 30 minutes to prevent them burning during cooking. Preheat the broiler to medium. Thread the chicken pieces and cherry tomatoes alternately onto the skewers and place on a broiler rack.

3 Spoon over any remaining glaze and cook under the preheated hot broiler for 8–10 minutes, turning occasionally, until the chicken is cooked through. Transfer to 4 large serving plates, garnish with a few sprigs of fresh rosemary, and serve with freshly cooked couscous or rice.

hot & spicy chicken with peanuts

ingredients

serves 4

marinade

2 tbsp soy sauce

1 tsp chili powder (or to taste)

stir-fry

12 oz/350 g skinless, boneless
    chicken breasts, cut into chunks

4 tbsp vegetable oil

1 garlic clove, finely chopped

1 tsp grated fresh ginger

3 shallots, thinly sliced

1½ cups carrots, thinly sliced

1 tsp white wine vinegar

pinch of sugar

3¼ oz/90 g/scant ⅔ cup
    roasted peanuts

1 tbsp peanut oil

cooked rice and cilantro sprigs,
    to serve

method

1 To make the marinade, mix the soy sauce and chili powder in a bowl. Add the chicken chunks and toss to coat. Cover with plastic wrap and refrigerate for 30 minutes.

2 Heat the vegetable oil in a wok or skillet, and stir-fry the chicken until browned and well cooked. Remove from the wok then set aside and keep warm.

3 If necessary, add a little more oil to the wok, then add the garlic, ginger, shallots, and carrots. Stir-fry for 2–3 minutes.

4 Return the chicken to the wok and fry until it is warmed through. Add the vinegar, sugar, and peanuts, then stir well and drizzle with the peanut oil.

5 Serve immediately with freshly cooked rice and cilantro sprigs.

chicken satay

ingredients

serves 4

2 tbsp vegetable or peanut oil
1 tbsp sesame oil
juice of 1/2 lime
2 skinless, boneless chicken
    breasts, cut into small cubes

dip

2 tbsp vegetable or peanut oil
1 small onion, finely chopped
1 small fresh green chile, seeded
    and chopped
1 garlic clove, finely chopped
4 oz/115 g/1/2 cup crunchy
    peanut butter
6–8 tbsp water
juice of 1/2 lime

method

1 Combine both the oils and the lime juice in a nonmetallic dish. Add the chicken cubes, cover with plastic wrap, and let chill for 1 hour. Soak 8–12 wooden skewers in cold water for 30 minutes before use, to prevent burning.

2 To make the dip, heat the oil in a skillet and sauté the onion, chile, and garlic over low heat, stirring occasionally, for about 5 minutes, until just softened. Add the peanut butter, water, and lime juice and let simmer gently, stirring constantly, until the peanut butter has softened enough to make a dip—you may need to add extra water to make a thinner consistency.

3 Meanwhile, drain the chicken cubes and thread them onto the wooden skewers. Put under a hot broiler or on a barbecue, turning frequently, for about 10 minutes, until cooked and browned. Serve hot with the warm dip.

five-spice chicken with vegetables

ingredients

serves 4

2 tbsp sesame oil

1 garlic clove, chopped

3 scallions, trimmed and sliced

1 tbsp cornstarch

2 tbsp rice wine

4 skinless, boneless chicken
    breasts, cut into strips

1 tbsp Chinese five-spice powder

1 tbsp grated fresh ginger

4 fl oz/125 ml/½ cup chicken stock

3½ oz/100 g baby corn cobs, sliced

10½ oz/300 g/3 cups beansprouts

finely chopped scallions,
    to garnish, optional

freshly cooked jasmine rice,
    to serve

method

1 Heat the oil in a preheated wok or large skillet. Add the garlic and scallions and stir-fry over medium-high heat for 1 minute.

2 In a bowl, mix together the cornstarch and rice wine, then add the mixture to the pan. Stir-fry for 1 minute, then add the chicken, five-spice powder, ginger, and chicken stock and cook for another 4 minutes. Add the corn cobs and cook for 2 minutes, then add the beansprouts and cook for another minute.

3 Remove from the heat, garnish with chopped scallions, if using, and serve with freshly cooked jasmine rice.

sweet-&-sour chicken

ingredients

serves 4–6

1 lb/450 g lean chicken meat, cubed

5 tbsp vegetable or peanut oil

½ tsp minced garlic

½ tsp finely chopped fresh ginger

1 green bell pepper, coarsely chopped

1 onion, coarsely chopped

1 carrot, finely sliced

1 tsp sesame oil

1 tbsp finely chopped scallion

freshly cooked rice, to serve

marinade

2 tsp light soy sauce

1 tsp Shaoxing rice wine

pinch of white pepper

½ tsp salt

dash of sesame oil

sauce

8 tbsp rice vinegar

4 tbsp sugar

2 tsp light soy sauce

6 tbsp tomato ketchup

method

1 Place all the marinade ingredients in a bowl and marinate the chicken pieces for at least 20 minutes.

2 To prepare the sauce, heat the vinegar in a pan and add the sugar, light soy sauce, and tomato ketchup. Stir to dissolve the sugar, then set aside.

3 In a preheated wok or deep pan, heat 3 tablespoons of the oil and stir-fry the chicken until it starts to turn golden brown. Remove and set aside.

4 In the clean wok or deep pan, heat the remaining oil and cook the garlic and ginger until fragrant. Add the vegetables and cook for 2 minutes. Add the chicken and cook for 1 minute. Finally add the sauce and sesame oil, then stir in the scallion and serve with rice.

chicken with bok choy

ingredients

serves 4

6 oz/175 g broccoli

1 tbsp peanut oil

1-inch/2.5-cm piece fresh ginger, finely grated

1 fresh red Thai chile, seeded and chopped

2 garlic cloves, crushed

1 red onion, cut into wedges

1 lb/450 g skinless, boneless chicken breast, cut into thin strips

6 oz/175 g bok choy, shredded

4 oz/115 g baby corn, halved

1 tbsp light soy sauce

1 tbsp Thai fish sauce

1 tbsp chopped fresh cilantro

1 tbsp toasted sesame seeds

method

1 Break the broccoli into small florets and cook in a pan of lightly salted boiling water for 3 minutes. Drain and set aside.

2 Heat a wok over high heat until almost smoking, add the oil, and then add the ginger, chile, and garlic. Stir-fry for 1 minute. Add the onion and chicken and stir-fry for an additional 3–4 minutes, or until the chicken is sealed on all sides.

3 Add the remaining vegetables to the wok, including the broccoli, and stir-fry for 3–4 minutes, or until tender.

4 Add the soy and Thai fish sauces to the wok and stir-fry for an additional 1–2 minutes, then serve at once sprinkled with the cilantro and sesame seeds.

creamy chicken curry with lemon rice

ingredients

serves 4

2 tbsp vegetable oil
4 skinless, boneless chicken
    breasts, 1 lb 12 oz/800 g, cut
    into 1-inch/2.5-cm pieces
1½ tsp cumin seeds
1 large onion, grated
2 fresh green chiles, finely chopped
2 large garlic cloves, grated
1 tbsp grated fresh ginger
1 tsp ground turmeric
1 tsp ground coriander
1 tsp garam masala
10 fl oz/300 ml/1¼ cups
    coconut milk
9 fl oz/250 ml chopped tomatoes
2 tsp lemon juice
2 tbsp chopped fresh cilantro,
    to garnish

lemon rice

12 oz/350 g/scant 1¾ cups
    basmati rice, rinsed
40 fl oz/1.25 liters/5 cups water
juice and grated rind of 1 lemon
3 cloves

method

1 Heat the oil in a large, heavy-bottom pan over medium heat. Add the chicken and cook for 5–8 minutes, until lightly browned and cooked through. Remove from the pan and set aside. Add the cumin seeds and cook until they start to darken and sizzle. Stir in the onion, partially cover, and cook over medium-low heat, stirring frequently, for 10 minutes, or until soft and golden. Add the chiles, garlic, ginger, turmeric, ground coriander, and garam masala and cook for 1 minute.

2 Return the chicken to the pan and stir in the coconut milk and tomatoes. Partially cover and cook for 15 minutes until the sauce has reduced and thickened. Stir in the lemon juice and season with salt.

3 Meanwhile, cook the rice. Put the rice into a pan and cover with the water. Add the lemon juice and cloves. Bring to a boil, then reduce the heat, cover, and let simmer over very low heat for 15 minutes, or until the rice is tender and all the water has been absorbed. Remove the pan from the heat and stir in the lemon rind. Let the rice stand, covered, for 5 minutes.

4 Serve the curry with the lemon rice, sprinkled with fresh cilantro.

thai green chicken curry

ingredients

serves 4

2 tbsp peanut or corn oil

2 tbsp Thai Green Curry Paste

1 lb 2 oz/500 g skinless, boneless
    chicken breasts, cut into cubes

2 kaffir lime leaves, roughly torn

1 lemongrass stalk, finely chopped

8 fl oz/225 ml/1 cup coconut milk

16 baby eggplants, halved

2 tbsp Thai fish sauce

sprigs of fresh Thai basil and thinly
    sliced kaffir lime leaves,
        to garnish

method

1 Heat the oil in a preheated wok or large, heavy-bottom skillet. Add the curry paste and stir-fry briefly until all the aromas are released.

2 Add the chicken, lime leaves, and lemongrass and stir-fry for 3–4 minutes, until the meat is beginning to color. Add the coconut milk and eggplants and simmer gently for 8–10 minutes, or until tender.

3 Stir in the fish sauce and serve immediately garnished with sprigs of Thai basil and lime leaves.

variation

Replace the baby eggplants with 3 green bell peppers, sliced, which will enhance the green color of the curry.

chicken breasts with coconut milk

ingredients

serves 4

1 small onion, chopped
1 fresh green chile, seeded
　　and chopped
1-inch/2.5-cm piece fresh
　　ginger, chopped
2 tsp ground coriander
1 tsp ground cumin
1 tsp fennel seeds
1 tsp ground star anise
1 tsp cardamom seeds
½ tsp ground turmeric
½ tsp black peppercorns
½ tsp ground cloves
20 fl oz/625 ml/2½ cups canned
　　coconut milk
4 skinless, boneless chicken
　　breasts
vegetable oil, for brushing
fresh cilantro sprigs, to garnish
tomato rice and naan bread,
　　to serve

method

1 Place the onion, chile, ginger, coriander, cumin, fennel seeds, star anise, cardamom seeds, turmeric, peppercorns, cloves, and 16 fl oz/500 ml/2 cups of the coconut milk in a food processor and process to make a paste, adding more coconut milk if necessary.

2 Using a sharp knife, slash the chicken breasts several times and place in a large, shallow, nonmetallic dish in a single layer. Pour over half the coconut milk mixture and turn to coat completely. Cover with plastic wrap and let marinate in the refrigerator for at least 1 hour, and up to 8 hours.

3 Heat a ridged grill pan and brush lightly with vegetable oil. Add the chicken, in batches if necessary, and cook for 6–7 minutes on each side, or until tender.

4 Meanwhile, pour the remaining coconut milk mixture into a pan and bring to a boil, stirring occasionally. Arrange the chicken in a warmed serving dish, spoon over a little of the coconut sauce, and garnish with cilantro sprigs. Serve hot with tomato rice and naan bread.

balti chicken

ingredients

serves 6

3 tbsp ghee or vegetable oil

2 large onions, sliced

3 tomatoes, sliced

½ tsp nigella seeds

4 black peppercorns

2 cardamom pods

1 cinnamon stick

1 tsp chili powder

1 tsp garam masala

1 tsp garlic paste

1 tsp ginger paste

salt

1 lb 9 oz/700 g skinless, boneless
    chicken breasts or thighs, diced

2 tbsp plain yogurt

2 tbsp chopped fresh cilantro,
    plus extra to garnish

2 fresh green chiles, seeded
    and finely chopped

2 tbsp lime juice

naan bread, to serve

method

1 Heat the ghee in a large, heavy-bottom skillet. Add the onions and cook over low heat, stirring occasionally, for 10 minutes, or until golden. Add the sliced tomatoes, kalonji seeds, peppercorns, cardamoms, cinnamon stick, chili powder, garam masala, garlic paste, and ginger paste and season with salt. Cook, stirring constantly, for 5 minutes.

2 Add the chicken and cook, stirring constantly, for 5 minutes, or until well coated in the spice paste. Stir in the yogurt. Cover and let simmer, stirring occasionally, for 10 minutes.

3 Stir in the chopped cilantro, chiles, and lime juice. Transfer to a warmed serving dish, sprinkle with more chopped cilantro, and serve immediately with naan bread.

lime chicken with mint

ingredients

serves 6

3 tbsp finely chopped fresh mint
4 tbsp honey
4 tbsp lime juice
salt and pepper
12 boneless chicken thighs
mixed salad, to serve

sauce

5 fl oz/150 ml/²⁄₃ cup
    lowfat thick plain yogurt
1 tbsp finely chopped
    fresh mint
2 tsp finely grated lime rind

method

1 Mix the mint, honey, and lime juice in a large bowl and season with salt and pepper. Use toothpicks to keep the chicken thighs in neat shapes and add the chicken to the marinade, turning to coat evenly.

2 Cover with plastic wrap and let the chicken marinate in the refrigerator for at least 30 minutes. Remove the chicken from the marinade and drain. Set aside the marinade.

3 Preheat the broiler to medium. Place the chicken on a broiler rack and cook under the hot broiler for 15–18 minutes, or until the chicken is tender and the juices run clear when the tip of a knife is inserted into the thickest part of the meat, turning the chicken frequently and basting with the marinade.

4 Meanwhile, combine all the sauce ingredients in a bowl. Remove the toothpicks and serve with a mixed salad and the sauce, for dipping.

chicken with sesame sauce

ingredients

serves 4

12 oz/350 g boneless, skinless
    chicken meat
few drops of sesame oil
2 tbsp sesame paste
1 tbsp light soy sauce
1 tbsp chicken stock
½ tsp salt
pinch of sugar
8 tbsp shredded lettuce leaves
1 tbsp sesame seeds, roasted,
    to serve

method

1 Place the chicken in a pan of cold water, then bring to a boil and let simmer for 8–10 minutes. Drain and let cool a little, then cut or tear the chicken into bite-size pieces.

2 Mix together the sesame oil, sesame paste, light soy sauce, chicken stock, salt, and sugar and whisk until the sauce is thick and smooth. Toss in the chicken.

3 To serve, put the shredded lettuce on a large plate and spoon the chicken and sauce on top. Sprinkle with the sesame seeds and serve at room temperature.

thai spiced chicken with zucchini

ingredients

serves 4

1 tbsp olive oil
1 garlic clove, finely chopped
1-inch/2.5-cm piece fresh ginger, peeled and finely chopped
1 small fresh red chile, seeded and finely chopped
12 oz/350 g skinless, boneless chicken breasts, cut into thin strips
1 tbsp Thai 7-spice seasoning
1 red bell pepper and 1 yellow bell pepper, seeded and sliced
2 zucchini, thinly sliced
8 oz/225 g canned bamboo shoots, drained
2 tbsp dry sherry or apple juice
1 tbsp light soy sauce
2 tbsp chopped fresh cilantro, plus extra to garnish
salt and pepper

method

1 Heat the olive oil in a nonstick wok or large skillet. Add the garlic, ginger, and chile and stir-fry for 30 seconds to release the flavors.

2 Add the chicken and Thai seasoning and stir-fry for about 4 minutes or until the chicken has colored all over. Add the peppers and zucchini and stir-fry for 1–2 minutes, or until slightly softened.

3 Stir in the bamboo shoots and stir-fry for another 2–3 minutes, or until the chicken is cooked through and tender. Add the sherry or apple juice, soy sauce, and seasoning and sizzle for 1–2 minutes.

4 Stir in the chopped cilantro and serve immediately, garnished with extra cilantro.

bacon-wrapped chicken burgers

ingredients

serves 4

1 lb/450 g fresh ground chicken
1 onion, grated
2 garlic cloves, crushed
2 oz/55 g/³⁄₈ cup pine nuts, toasted
2 oz/55 g Gruyère cheese, grated
2 tbsp fresh snipped chives
2 tbsp whole wheat flour
8 lean Canadian bacon slices
1–2 tbsp corn oil
salt and pepper
mayonnaise and chopped scallions
    (green part only), to garnish
crusty rolls, chopped lettuce and
    red onion rings, to serve

method

1 Place the ground chicken, onion, garlic, pine nuts, cheese, chives, and salt and pepper in a food processor. Using the pulse button, blend the mixture together using short sharp bursts. Scrape out onto a board and shape into 4 even-size burgers. Coat in the flour, then cover and let chill for 1 hour.

2 Wrap each burger with 2 bacon slices, securing in place with a wooden toothpick.

3 Heat a heavy-bottom skillet and add the oil. When hot, add the burgers and cook over medium heat for 5–6 minutes on each side, or until thoroughly cooked through.

4 Serve the burgers immediately in crusty rolls on a bed of lettuce and red onion rings and top with mayonnaise and scallions.

chicken fajitas

ingredients

serves 4

3 tbsp olive oil, plus extra
   for drizzling
3 tbsp maple syrup or honey
1 tbsp red wine vinegar
2 garlic cloves, crushed
2 tsp dried oregano
1–2 tsp dried chili flakes
4 skinless, boneless chicken breasts
2 red bell peppers, seeded and cut
   into 1-inch/2.5-cm strips
8 flour tortillas, warmed
salt and pepper
guacamole, to serve

method

1 Place the oil, maple syrup, vinegar, garlic, oregano, chili flakes, salt, and pepper in a large, shallow plate or bowl and mix together.

2 Slice the chicken across the grain into slices 1 inch/ 2.5 cm thick. Toss in the marinade until well coated. Cover and let chill in the refrigerator for 2–3 hours, turning occasionally.

3 Heat a grill pan until hot. Lift the chicken slices from the marinade with a slotted spoon, lay on the grill pan, and cook over medium-high heat for 3–4 minutes on each side, or until cooked through. Remove the chicken to a warmed serving plate and keep warm.

4 Add the bell peppers, skin-side down, to the grill pan, and cook for 2 minutes on each side. Transfer to the serving plate.

5 Serve at once with guacamole, in the warmed tortillas.

chicken wraps

ingredients

serves 4

5 fl oz/150 ml/generous
⅔ cup lowfat plain yogurt
1 tbsp whole-grain mustard
10 oz/280 g cooked skinless,
boneless chicken breast, diced
5 oz/140 g iceberg lettuce, finely
shredded
3 oz/85 g cucumber, thinly sliced
2 celery stalks, sliced
3 oz/85 g/½ cup black seedless
grapes, halved
8 x 8-inch/20-cm soft flour
tortillas or 4 x 10-inch/
25-cm soft flour tortillas
pepper

method

1 Combine the yogurt and mustard in a bowl and season with pepper. Stir in the chicken and toss until thoroughly coated.

2 Put the lettuce, cucumber, celery, and grapes into a separate bowl and mix well.

3 Fold a tortilla in half and in half again to make a cone that is easy to hold. Half-fill the tortilla pocket with the salad mixture and top with some of the chicken mixture. Repeat with the remaining tortillas, salad, and chicken. Serve at once.

filo chicken pie

ingredients

serves 6–8

3 lb 5 oz/1.5 kg whole chicken

1 small onion, halved, and 3 large
　onions, finely chopped

1 carrot, thickly sliced

1 celery stalk, thickly sliced

pared zest of 1 lemon

1 bay leaf

10 peppercorns

5½ oz/155 g butter

2 oz/55 g/scant ½ cup
　all-purpose flour

5 fl oz/150 ml/⅔ cup milk

1 oz/25 g/⅓ cup kefalotiri or
　romano cheese, grated

3 eggs, beaten

8 oz/225 g filo pastry (work with
　one sheet at a time and keep
　the remaining sheets covered
　with a damp dish towel)

salt and pepper

method

1 Put the chicken in a large pan with the halved onion, carrot, celery, lemon zest, bay leaf, and peppercorns. Add cold water to cover and bring to a boil. Cover and simmer for about 1 hour, or until the chicken is cooked.

2 Remove the chicken and set aside to cool. Bring the stock to a boil and boil until reduced to about 20 fl oz/ 625 ml/2½ cups. Strain and reserve the stock. Cut the cooled chicken into pieces, without the skin and bones.

3 Fry the chopped onions until softened in 2 oz/55 g of the butter. Add the flour and cook gently, stirring, for 1–2 minutes. Gradually stir in the reserved stock and the milk. Bring to a boil, stirring constantly, then simmer for 1–2 minutes until thick and smooth. Remove from the heat, add the chicken, and season. Let cool, then stir in the cheese and eggs.

4 Melt the remaining butter and use a little to grease a deep 12 x 8-inch/30 x 20-cm metal baking pan. Cut the pastry sheets in half widthwise. Line the pan with one sheet of pastry and brush it with melted butter. Repeat with half of the pastry sheets. Spread the filling over the pastry, then top with the pastry sheets, brushing each with butter and tucking down the edges.

5 Bake in a preheated oven, 375°F/190°C, for about 50 minutes, until golden. Serve warm.

pan-fried chicken & cilantro

ingredients

serves 4

1 tbsp corn oil

4 skinless, boneless chicken
   breasts, about 4 oz/115 g each,
   trimmed of all visible fat

1 tsp cornstarch

1 tbsp water

3 fl oz/90 ml/⅓ cup lowfat plain
   yogurt

2 tbsp reduced fat light cream

6 fl oz/175 ml/¾ cup chicken stock

2 tbsp lime juice

2 garlic cloves, finely chopped

1 shallot, finely chopped

1 tomato, peeled, seeded,
   and chopped

1 bunch of fresh cilantro, coarsely
   chopped, with extra to garnish

salt and pepper

method

1 Heat the corn oil in a heavy-bottom skillet, add the chicken and cook over medium heat for 5 minutes on each side, or until the juices run clear when the meat is pierced with the tip of a sharp knife. Remove from the skillet and keep warm.

2 Mix the cornstarch and water until smooth. Stir in the yogurt and cream. Pour the chicken stock and lime juice into the skillet and add the garlic and shallot. Reduce the heat and let simmer for 1 minute. Stir the tomato into the yogurt mixture and stir the mixture into the skillet. Season with salt and pepper. Cook, stirring constantly, for 1–2 minutes, or until slightly thickened, but do not let the mixture boil. Stir in the chopped fresh cilantro.

3 Place the chicken on a large serving plate, pour the sauce over it and garnish with the reserved cilantro sprigs. Serve.

chicken kabobs with yogurt sauce

ingredients

serves 4

10 fl oz/300 ml/1¼ cups strained
  plain yogurt
2 garlic cloves, crushed
juice of ½ lemon
1 tbsp chopped fresh herbs such
  as oregano, dill, tarragon,
  or parsley
4 large skinless, boneless chicken
  breasts
oil, for oiling
8 firm stems of fresh rosemary,
  optional
salt and pepper
lemon wedges, to garnish
shredded romaine lettuce
  and rice, to serve

method

1 To make the sauce, put the yogurt, garlic, lemon juice, herbs, salt, and pepper in a large bowl and mix well together.

2 Cut the chicken breasts into chunks measuring about 1½ inches/4 cm square. Add to the yogurt mixture and toss well together until the chicken pieces are coated. Cover and leave to marinate in the refrigerator for about 1 hour. If you are using wooden skewers, soak them in cold water for 30 minutes before use.

3 Preheat the broiler. Thread the pieces of chicken onto 8 flat, oiled, metal kabob skewers, wooden skewers, or rosemary stems and place on an oiled broiler pan.

4 Cook the kabobs under the broiler for about 15 minutes, turning and basting with the remaining marinade occasionally, until lightly browned and tender.

5 Pour the remaining marinade into a pan and heat gently but do not boil. Serve the kabobs with shredded lettuce on a bed of rice and garnish with lemon wedges. Accompany with the yogurt sauce.

gingered chicken kabobs

ingredients

serves 4

3 skinless, boneless chicken
    breasts, cut into small cubes
juice of 1 lime
1-inch/2.5-cm piece ginger,
    peeled and chopped
1 fresh red chile, seeded
    and sliced
2 tbsp vegetable or peanut oil
1 onion, sliced
2 garlic cloves, chopped
1 eggplant, cut into chunks
2 zucchini, cut into thick slices
1 red bell pepper, seeded and
    cut into squares
2 tbsp red curry paste
2 tbsp Thai soy sauce
1 tsp jaggery or soft light brown
    sugar
boiled rice, with chopped cilantro,
    to serve

method

1 Put the chicken cubes in a shallow dish. Mix the lime, ginger, and chile together and pour over the chicken pieces. Stir gently to coat. Cover and let chill in the refrigerator for at least 3 hours to marinate.

2 Soak 8–12 wooden skewers in cold water for 30 minutes before use, to prevent burning.

3 Thread the chicken pieces onto the soaked wooden skewers and cook under a hot broiler for 3–4 minutes, turning frequently, until they are cooked through.

4 Meanwhile, heat the oil in a wok or large skillet and sauté the onion and garlic for 1–2 minutes, until softened, but not browned. Add the eggplant, zucchini, and bell pepper and cook for 3–4 minutes, until cooked but still firm. Add the curry paste, soy sauce, and sugar, and cook for 1 minute.

5 Divide the vegetables among serving plates and top with the kabobs. Serve hot with boiled rice, stirred through with chopped cilantro.

asian-style glazed chicken wings

ingredients

serves 4

8 chicken wings, each wing
chopped into 3 pieces
5 tbsp peanut oil
6 tbsp chicken stock or water
2 tbsp chopped fresh cilantro

marinade

1½ tbsp Chinese rice wine
or dry sherry
1 tbsp soy sauce
1 tbsp rice vinegar
1½ tbsp sugar
¾ tsp salt
⅛ tsp Chinese five-spice seasoning
3 tbsp hoisin sauce
1 tsp finely chopped fresh ginger

method

1 To make the marinade, combine the wine, soy sauce, and vinegar in a small bowl. Add the sugar, salt, and five-spice seasoning and stir until dissolved. Mix in the hoisin sauce and ginger.

2 Put the chopped chicken wings in a shallow dish and pour in the marinade, turning the wings to coat. Let stand to marinate for 1 hour at room temperature, or overnight in the refrigerator.

3 Heat a wok over a high heat, add the oil, and when it is almost smoking, add the chicken wings and marinade. Stir-fry for 5 minutes, then sprinkle with 4 tablespoons of the stock and stir-fry for another 4 minutes.

4 Using tongs, transfer the wings to a serving dish and sprinkle with the cilantro. Pour off and discard most of the oil from the wok and return to the heat. Add the remaining 2 tablespoons of stock and stir with a wooden spoon until blended, scraping up the sticky sediment. Pour into a small bowl and serve with the wings as a dipping sauce.

hearty dishes

traditional roast chicken

ingredients

serves 4

1 oz/25 g butter, softened

1 garlic clove, finely chopped

3 tbsp finely chopped
toasted walnuts

1 tbsp chopped fresh parsley

salt and pepper

1 oven-ready chicken, weighing
4 lb/1.8 kg

1 lime, cut into fourths

2 tbsp vegetable oil

1 tbsp cornstarch

2 tbsp water

lime wedges and fresh rosemary
sprigs, to garnish

roast potatoes and a selection
of freshly cooked vegetables,
to serve

method

1 Mix 1 tablespoon of the butter with the garlic, walnuts, and parsley together in a small bowl. Season well with salt and pepper. Loosen the skin from the breast of the chicken without breaking it. Spread the butter mixture evenly between the skin and breast meat. Place the lime fourths inside the body cavity.

2 Pour the oil into a roasting pan. Transfer the chicken to the pan and dot the skin with the remaining butter. Roast in a preheated oven, 375°F/190°C, for 1¾ hours, basting occasionally, until the chicken is tender and the juices run clear when a skewer is inserted into the thickest part of the meat. Lift out the chicken and place on a serving platter to rest for 10 minutes.

3 Blend the cornstarch with the water, then stir into the juices in the pan. Stir over low heat until thickened, adding more water if necessary. Garnish the chicken with lime wedges and rosemary sprigs. Serve with roast potatoes and a selection of freshly cooked vegetables and spoon over the thickened juices.

chicken & barley stew

ingredients

serves 4

2 tbsp vegetable oil

8 small, skinless chicken thighs

generous 2 cups chicken stock

scant ½ cup pearl barley, rinsed
and drained

7 oz/200 g small new potatoes,
scrubbed and cut in half
lengthwise

2 large carrots, peeled and sliced

1 leek, trimmed and sliced

2 shallots, sliced

1 tbsp tomato paste

1 bay leaf

1 zucchini, trimmed and sliced

2 tbsp chopped fresh flat-leaf
parsley, plus extra sprigs
to garnish

2 tbsp all-purpose flour

4 tbsp water

salt and pepper

method

1 Heat the oil in a large pot over medium heat. Add the chicken and cook for 3 minutes, then turn over and cook on the other side for another 2 minutes. Add the stock, barley, potatoes, carrots, leek, shallots, tomato paste, and bay leaf. Bring to a boil, lower the heat, and simmer for 30 minutes.

2 Add the zucchini and chopped parsley, cover the pan, and cook for another 20 minutes, or until the chicken is cooked through. Remove the bay leaf and discard.

3 In a separate bowl, mix the flour with the water and stir into a smooth paste. Add it to the stew and cook, stirring, over low heat for another 5 minutes. Season to taste with salt and pepper.

4 Remove from the heat, ladle into individual serving bowls, and garnish with sprigs of fresh parsley.

chicken, tomato & onion casserole

ingredients

serves 4

1½ tbsp unsalted butter
2 tbsp olive oil
4 lb/1.8 kg skinned chicken
    drumsticks
2 red onions, sliced
2 garlic cloves, finely chopped
14 oz/400 g canned chopped
    tomatoes
2 tbsp chopped flat-leaf parsley,
    plus extra to garnish
6 fresh basil leaves, torn
1 tbsp sun-dried tomato paste
⅔ cup full-bodied red wine
3¼ cups sliced mushrooms
salt and pepper

method

1 Heat the butter with the olive oil in a large flameproof casserole. Add the chicken drumsticks and cook, turning frequently, for 5–10 minutes, or until golden all over and sealed. Using a slotted spoon, transfer the drumsticks to a plate.

2 Add the onions and garlic to the casserole and cook over low heat, stirring occasionally, for 10 minutes, or until golden. Add the tomatoes, parsley, basil, tomato paste, and wine, and then season to taste with salt and pepper.

3 Bring to a boil, then return the chicken drumsticks to the casserole, pushing them down under the liquid. Cover and cook in a preheated oven, 325°F/160°C, for 50 minutes.

4 Add the mushrooms and cook for another 10 minutes, or until the chicken drumsticks are tender and the juices run clear when a skewer is inserted into the thickest part of the meat. Serve immediately, garnished with chopped parsley.

spiced chicken stew

ingredients

serves 6

4 lb/1.8 kg chicken parts

2 tbsp paprika

2 tbsp olive oil

2 tbsp butter

1 lb/450 g onions, chopped

2 yellow bell peppers, seeded
and chopped

14 oz/400 g canned chopped
tomatoes

8 fl oz/225 ml/scant 1 cup dry
white wine

16 fl oz/450 ml/generous 1¾ cups
chicken stock

1 tbsp Worcestershire sauce

½ tsp Tabasco sauce

1 tbsp finely chopped fresh parsley

11½ oz/325 g canned corn kernels,
drained

15 oz/425 g canned lima beans,
drained and rinsed

2 tbsp all-purpose flour

4 tbsp water

salt

fresh parsley sprigs, to garnish

method

1 Season the chicken parts with salt and dust with paprika.

2 Heat the oil and butter in a flameproof casserole or large pan. Add the chicken parts and cook over medium heat, turning, for 10–15 minutes, or until golden. Transfer to a plate with a slotted spoon.

3 Add the onion and bell peppers to the casserole. Cook over low heat, stirring occasionally, for 5 minutes, or until softened.

4 Add the tomatoes, wine, stock, Worcestershire sauce, Tabasco sauce, and parsley and bring to a boil, stirring. Return the chicken to the casserole, cover, and simmer, stirring occasionally, for 30 minutes.

5 Add the corn and beans to the casserole, partially re-cover, and simmer for an additional 30 minutes. Place the flour and water in a small bowl and mix to make a paste. Stir a ladleful of the cooking liquid into the paste, then stir the paste into the stew. Cook, stirring frequently, for 5 minutes. Serve, garnished with parsley.

roasted chicken with sun-blush tomato pesto

ingredients

serves 4

4 skinless, boneless chicken
    breasts, about 1 lb 12 oz/
    800 g in total
1 tbsp olive oil
salt and pepper
2 tbsp pine nuts, lightly toasted,
    to garnish

pesto

4½ oz/125 g sun-blush tomatoes
    in oil (drained weight),
    chopped
2 garlic cloves, crushed
4 tbsp pine nuts, lightly toasted
5 fl oz/150 ml/⅔ cup extra virgin
    olive oil

method

1 To make the red pesto, put the sun-blush tomatoes, garlic, 4 tablespoons of the pine nuts, and oil into a food processor and process to a coarse paste.

2 Arrange the chicken in a large, ovenproof dish or roasting pan. Brush each breast with the oil, then place a tablespoon of red pesto over each breast. Using the back of a spoon, spread the pesto so that it covers the top of each breast. (Store the remaining pesto in an airtight container in the refrigerator for up to 1 week.)

3 Roast the chicken in a preheated oven, 400°F/200°C for 30 minutes, or until tender and the juices run clear when a skewer is inserted into the thickest part of the meat.

4 Serve sprinkled with toasted pine nuts.

variation

Add 12 stoned and finely chopped black olives (well drained and rinsed) and ½ tablespoon olive oil to the pesto after processing; stir well.

roast cinnamon squab chickens with lentils

ingredients

serves 4

4 squab chickens, about
    1 lb 2 oz/500 g each
2 tbsp maple syrup
1 tsp ground cinnamon
1 tbsp vegetable oil
3½ fl oz/100 ml/generous ⅓ cup
    low-salt chicken stock
2 red onions, sliced
1 tsp cumin seeds
1 tsp coriander seeds
1 tbsp olive oil
2 garlic cloves, crushed
1 lb 12 oz/800 g canned lentils,
    drained and rinsed
1 tbsp unsalted butter
2 tbsp chopped fresh parsley
pepper
steamed broccoli or green beans,
    to serve (optional)

method

1 Arrange the squab chickens in a roasting pan. Mix the maple syrup, cinnamon, and vegetable oil together in a small bowl and brush over the breasts of the squab chickens. Pour the stock into the roasting pan and tuck the onion slices around the birds. Roast in a preheated oven, 375°F/190°C, for 35 minutes.

2 Meanwhile, heat a nonstick skillet over medium heat, add the cumin and coriander seeds, and cook, turning, until they start to give off an aroma. Tip into a mortar and finely crush with a pestle.

3 Heat the olive oil in a skillet over low heat, add the garlic and spices, and cook for 1–2 minutes, stirring constantly. Add the lentils and cook for 10–15 minutes, stirring occasionally.

4 Remove the chicken from the oven, and keep warm. Put the roasting pan on the stove and bring the cooking juices up to a simmer. Stir in the butter and half the parsley. Season with pepper.

5 To serve, divide the lentils among 4 warmed serving plates. Add a squab chicken to each plate, pour over the sauce, and sprinkle with the remaining parsley. Serve with steamed broccoli or green beans, if liked.

sticky lime chicken

ingredients

serves 4

4 part-boned, skinless chicken
    breasts, about 5 oz/140 g each
grated rind and juice of 1 lime
1 tbsp honey
1 tbsp olive oil
1 garlic clove, chopped (optional)
1 tbsp chopped fresh thyme
pepper
boiled new potatoes and
    lightly cooked seasonal
    vegetables, to serve

method

1 Arrange the chicken breasts in a shallow roasting pan.

2 Put the lime rind and juice, honey, oil, garlic, if using, and thyme in a small bowl and combine thoroughly. Spoon the mixture evenly over the chicken breasts and season with pepper.

3 Roast the chicken in a preheated oven, 375°F/190°C, basting every 10 minutes, for 35–40 minutes, or until the chicken is tender and the juices run clear when a skewer is inserted into the thickest part of the meat. If the juices still run pink, return the chicken to the oven and cook for an additional 5 minutes, then test again. As the chicken cooks, the liquid in the pan thickens to give a tasty, sticky coating.

4 Serve with boiled new potatoes and lightly cooked seasonal vegetables.

chicken with saffron mash potatoes

ingredients

serves 4

1 lb 4 oz/550 g mealy potatoes,
   cut into chunks
1 garlic clove, peeled
1 tsp saffron threads, crushed
40 fl oz/1.25 liters/5 cups chicken
   or vegetable stock
4 skinless, boneless chicken
   breasts, trimmed of all
   visible fat
2 tbsp olive oil
1 tbsp lemon juice
1 tbsp chopped fresh thyme
1 tbsp chopped fresh cilantro
1 tbsp coriander seeds, crushed
3½ fl oz/100 ml/⅓ cup hot skim milk
salt and pepper
fresh thyme sprigs, to garnish

method

1 Put the potatoes, garlic, and saffron in a large heavy-bottom pan, add the stock and bring to a boil. Cover and let simmer for 20 minutes, or until tender.

2 Meanwhile, brush the chicken breasts all over with half the olive oil and all of the lemon juice. Sprinkle with the fresh thyme, cilantro, and the crushed coriander seeds. Heat a griddle pan, add the chicken, and cook over medium–high heat for 5 minutes on each side, or until the juices run clear when the meat is pierced with the tip of a sharp knife. Alternatively, cook the chicken breasts under a preheated medium-hot broiler for 5 minutes on each side, or until cooked through.

3 Drain the potatoes and return the contents of the strainer to the pan. Add the remaining olive oil and the milk, season with salt and pepper, and mash until smooth. Divide the saffron mash among 4 large, warmed serving plates, top with a piece of chicken, and garnish with a few sprigs of fresh thyme. Serve.

tarragon chicken

ingredients

serves 4

4 skinless, boneless chicken
    breasts, about 6 oz/175 g each
4 fl oz/125 ml/½ cup
    dry white wine
8–10 fl oz/250–300 ml/
    1–1¼ cups chicken stock
1 garlic clove, finely chopped
1 tbsp dried tarragon
6 fl oz/175 ml/¾ cup heavy cream
1 tbsp chopped fresh tarragon
salt and pepper
fresh tarragon sprigs, to garnish

method

1 Season the chicken with salt and pepper and place in a single layer in a large, heavy-bottom skillet. Pour in the wine and just enough chicken stock to cover, and add the garlic and dried tarragon. Bring to a boil, reduce the heat, and cook gently for 10 minutes, or until the chicken is tender and cooked through.

2 Remove the chicken with a slotted spoon or tongs, cover, and keep warm. Strain the poaching liquid into a clean skillet and skim off any fat from the surface. Bring to a boil and cook for 12–15 minutes, or until reduced by about two-thirds.

3 Stir in the cream, return to a boil, and cook until reduced by about half. Stir in the fresh tarragon. Slice the chicken breasts and arrange on warmed plates. Spoon over the sauce, garnish with tarragon sprigs, and serve immediately.

tuscan chicken

ingredients

serves 4

2 tbsp all-purpose flour

4 skinned chicken parts

3 tbsp olive oil

1 red onion, chopped

2 garlic cloves, finely chopped

1 red bell pepper, seeded and
    chopped

pinch of saffron threads

5 fl oz/150 ml/²/₃ cup chicken stock
    or a mixture of chicken stock
    and dry white wine

14 oz/400 g canned tomatoes,
    chopped

4 sun-dried tomatoes in oil,
    drained and chopped

8 oz/225 g portobello mushrooms,
    sliced

4 oz/115 g/²/₃ cup black olives,
    pitted

4 tbsp lemon juice

salt and pepper

fresh basil leaves, to garnish

tagliatelle, fettuccine, or tagliarini
    and crusty bread, to serve

method

1 Place the flour on a shallow plate and season with salt and pepper. Coat the chicken in the seasoned flour, shaking off any excess. Heat the olive oil in a large, flameproof casserole. Add the chicken and cook over medium heat, turning frequently, for 5–7 minutes, until golden brown. Remove from the casserole and set aside.

2 Add the onion, garlic, and red bell pepper to the casserole, reduce the heat and cook, stirring occasionally, for 5 minutes, until softened. Meanwhile, stir the saffron into the stock.

3 Stir the tomatoes, with the juice from the can, and the sun-dried tomatoes, mushrooms, and olives into the casserole and cook, stirring occasionally, for 3 minutes. Pour in the stock and saffron mixture and the lemon juice. Bring to a boil, then return the chicken to the casserole.

4 Cover and cook in a preheated oven, 350°F/180°C, for 1 hour, until the chicken is tender. Garnish with the basil leaves and serve immediately with pasta and crusty bread.

chicken with goat cheese & basil

ingredients

serves 4

4 skinless, boneless chicken breasts
3½ oz/100 g soft goat cheese
small bunch fresh basil
2 tbsp olive oil
salt and pepper

method

1 Using a sharp knife, slit along one long edge of each chicken breast, then carefully open out each breast to make a small pocket. Divide the cheese equally among the pockets, and tuck three or four basil leaves in each. Close the openings and season the breasts with salt and pepper.

2 Heat the oil in a skillet, add the chicken breasts, and fry gently for 15–20 minutes, turning several times, until golden and tender.

3 Serve warm, garnished with a sprig of basil.

chicken gumbo

ingredients

serves 4–6

3 lb 5 oz/1.5 kg chicken,
    cut into 6 parts

2 celery stalks, 1 broken in half
    and 1 finely chopped

1 carrot, chopped

2 onions, 1 sliced and 1 chopped

2 bay leaves

4 tbsp peanut oil

1¾ oz/50 g/⅓ cup all-purpose flour

2 large garlic cloves, crushed

1 green bell pepper, seeded
    and diced

1 lb/450 g fresh okra, trimmed,
    then cut crosswise into
    ½-inch/1-cm slices

8 oz/225 g andouille sausage
    or Polish kielbasa, sliced

2 tbsp tomato paste

1 tsp dried thyme

½ tsp cayenne pepper

14 oz/400 g canned peeled
    plum tomatoes

salt and pepper

cooked long-grain rice, to serve

method

1 Put the chicken into a large pan with water to cover, bring to the boil, skimming the surface to remove the foam. Reduce the heat to medium, add the celery stalk halves, carrot, sliced onion, 1 bay leaf, and ¼ teaspoon of salt and simmer for 30 minutes, or until the chicken is tender and the juices run clear when a skewer is inserted into the thickest part of the meat. Remove the chicken, straining and reserving 4 cups of the liquid. Remove and discard the skin, bones, and other ingredients. Cut the chicken flesh into bite-size pieces and reserve.

2 Heat the oil in a large pan. Over a low heat, sprinkle in the flour, and stir to make a roux. Add the chopped celery, chopped onion, garlic, green bell pepper, and okra to the pan. Increase the heat to medium–high and cook, stirring frequently, for 5 minutes. Add the sausage and cook, stirring frequently, for 2 minutes. Stir in all the remaining ingredients, except the chicken, including the second bay leaf and the reserved cooking liquid.

3 Bring to a boil, then reduce the heat to medium–low and simmer, uncovered, for 30 minutes, stirring occasionally. Add the chicken to the pan and simmer for another 30 minutes. Taste and adjust the seasoning, if necessary. Remove and discard the bay leaf, spoon the gumbo over the rice, and serve.

chicken in white wine

ingredients

serves 4

4 tbsp butter

2 tbsp olive oil

2 slices rindless, thick bacon, chopped

4 oz/115 g pearl onions, peeled

1 garlic clove, finely chopped

4 lb/1.8 kg chicken parts

14 fl oz/400 ml/1¾ cups dry white wine

10 fl oz/300 ml/1¼ cups chicken stock

1 bouquet garni

4 oz/115 g button mushrooms

1 oz/25 g/3 tbsp all-purpose flour

salt and pepper

fresh mixed herbs, to garnish

method

1 Melt half the butter with the oil in a flameproof casserole. Add the bacon and cook over medium heat, stirring, for 5–10 minutes, or until golden brown. Transfer the bacon to a large plate. Add the onions and garlic to the casserole and cook over low heat, stirring occasionally, for 10 minutes, or until golden. Transfer to the plate.

2 Add the chicken and cook over medium heat, stirring continuously, for 8–10 minutes, or until golden. Transfer to the plate. Drain off any excess fat. Stir in the wine and stock and bring to a boil, scraping any sediment off the bottom. Add the bouquet garni and season to taste with salt and pepper. Return the bacon, onions, and chicken to the casserole. Cover and cook in a preheated oven, 325°F/160°C, for 1 hour. Add the mushrooms, re-cover, and cook for 15 minutes. Meanwhile, make a beurre manié by mashing the remaining butter with the flour in a small bowl.

3 Remove the casserole from the oven and set over medium heat. Remove and discard the bouquet garni. Whisk in the beurre manié, a little at a time. Bring to a boil, stirring, then serve, garnished with fresh herb sprigs.

chicken tagine

ingredients

serves 4

1 tbsp olive oil

1 onion, cut into small wedges

2–4 garlic cloves, sliced

1 lb/450 g skinless, boneless chicken breasts, diced

1 tsp ground cumin

2 cinnamon sticks, lightly bruised

1 tbsp plain whole-wheat flour

8 oz/225 g/2¾ cups diced eggplant

1 red bell pepper, seeded and chopped

3 oz/85 g/1¼ cups sliced button mushrooms

1 tbsp tomato paste

1 pint/600 ml/2½ cups chicken stock

10 oz/280 g canned chickpeas, drained and rinsed

2 oz/55 g/⅓ cup chopped dried apricots

salt and pepper

1 tbsp chopped fresh cilantro, to garnish

method

1 Heat the oil in a large saucepan over medium heat, add the onion and garlic, and cook for 3 minutes, stirring frequently. Add the chicken and cook, stirring continuously, for another 5 minutes, or until sealed on all sides. Add the cumin and cinnamon sticks to the saucepan halfway through sealing the chicken.

2 Sprinkle in the flour and cook, stirring continuously, for 2 minutes. Add the eggplant, red bell pepper, and mushrooms and cook for another 2 minutes, stirring continuously. Blend the tomato paste with the stock, stir into the saucepan, and bring to a boil. Reduce the heat and add the chickpeas and apricots. Cover and simmer for 15–20 minutes, or until the chicken is tender.

3 Season with salt and pepper to taste and serve immediately, sprinkled with cilantro.

florida chicken

ingredients

serves 4

1 lb/450 g skinless, boneless
   chicken
1½ tbsp all-purpose flour
1 tbsp olive oil
1 onion, cut into wedges
2 celery stalks, sliced
5 fl oz/150 ml/⅔ cup orange juice
10 fl oz/300 ml/1¼ cups chicken
   stock
1 tbsp light soy sauce
1–2 tsp honey
1 tbsp grated orange rind
1 orange bell pepper, seeded
   and chopped
1 medium zucchini, sliced into
   half moons
2 small corn cobs, halved
1 orange, peeled and segmented
salt and pepper
1 tbsp chopped fresh parsley,
   to garnish

method

1 Lightly rinse the chicken and pat dry with paper towels. Cut into bite-size pieces. Season the flour well with salt and pepper. Toss the chicken in the seasoned flour until well coated and reserve any remaining seasoned flour.

2 Heat the oil in a large heavy-bottom skillet and cook the chicken over high heat, stirring frequently, for 5 minutes, or until golden on all sides and sealed. Using a slotted spoon, transfer the chicken to a plate. Add the onion and celery to the skillet and cook over medium heat, stirring frequently, for 5 minutes, or until softened. Sprinkle in the reserved seasoned flour and cook, stirring continuously, for 2 minutes, then remove from the heat. Gradually stir in the orange juice, stock, soy sauce, and honey, followed by the orange rind, then return to the heat and bring to a boil, stirring.

3 Return the chicken to the skillet. Reduce the heat, cover, and simmer, stirring occasionally, for 15 minutes. Add the orange pepper, zucchini, and corn cobs and simmer for another 10 minutes, or until the chicken and vegetables are tender. Add the orange segments, stir well, and heat for 1 minute. Serve, garnished with the parsley.

mexican chicken, chili & potato pot

ingredients

serves 4

2 tbsp vegetable oil

1 lb/450 g skinless, boneless
    chicken breasts, cubed

1 onion, finely chopped

1 green bell pepper, seeded
    and finely chopped

1 potato, diced

1 sweet potato, diced

2 garlic cloves, very finely chopped

1–2 fresh green chiles, seeded
    and finely chopped

7 oz/200 g canned chopped
    tomatoes

½ tsp dried oregano

½ tsp salt

¼ tsp pepper

4 tbsp chopped fresh cilantro

2 cups chicken stock

method

1 Heat the oil in a large heavy-bottom saucepan over medium–high heat. Add the chicken and cook until lightly browned. Reduce the heat to medium. Add the onion, bell pepper, potato, and sweet potato. Cover and cook, stirring occasionally, for 5 minutes, or until the vegetables begin to soften.

2 Add the garlic and chiles and cook for 1 minute. Stir in the tomatoes, oregano, salt, pepper, and half the cilantro and cook for 1 minute. Pour in the stock. Bring to a boil, then cover and simmer over a medium–low heat for 15–20 minutes, or until the chicken is cooked through and the vegetables are tender.

3 Sprinkle with the remaining cilantro just before serving.

coq au vin

ingredients

serves 4

2 tbsp butter
8 baby onions
4½ oz/125 g bacon,
    roughly chopped
4 chicken parts
1 garlic clove, finely chopped
12 white mushrooms
10 fl oz/300 ml/1¼ cups red wine
bouquet garni sachet
1 tbsp chopped fresh tarragon
salt and pepper
2 tsp cornstarch
1–2 tbsp cold water
fresh flat-leaf parsley
    sprigs, to garnish
sautéed sliced potatoes,
    to serve

method

1 Melt half of the butter in a large skillet over medium heat. Add the onions and bacon and cook, stirring, for 3 minutes. Lift out the bacon and onions and reserve.

2 Melt the remaining butter in the skillet and add the chicken parts. Cook for 3 minutes, then turn over and cook on the other side for 2 minutes. Drain off some of the chicken fat, then return the bacon and onions to the pan. Add the garlic, mushrooms, red wine, bouquet garni, and tarragon. Season with salt and pepper. Cook for about 1 hour, or until the chicken is cooked through.

3 Remove the skillet from the heat, lift out the chicken, onions, bacon, and mushrooms, transfer them to a serving platter, and keep the dish warm. Discard the bouquet garni.

4 Mix the cornstarch with enough of the water to make a paste, then stir into the juices in the skillet. Bring to a boil, reduce the heat, and cook, stirring, for 1 minute. Pour the sauce over the chicken, garnish with parsley sprigs, and serve with sautéed sliced potatoes.

spanish chicken with preserved lemons

ingredients

serves 4

1 tbsp all-purpose flour
4 chicken quarters, skin on
2 tbsp olive oil
2 garlic cloves, crushed
1 large Spanish onion, thinly sliced
24 fl oz/750 ml/3 cups
    low-salt chicken stock
½ tsp saffron threads
2 yellow bell peppers, seeded
    and cut into chunks
2 preserved lemons, cut into
    fourths
9 oz/250 g/generous 1¼ cups
    brown basmati rice
white pepper
12 pimiento-stuffed green olives
chopped fresh parsley,
    to garnish
salad greens, to serve

method

1 Put the flour into a large freezer bag. Add the chicken, close the top of the bag, and shake to coat with flour.

2 Heat the oil in a large skillet over low heat, add the garlic, and cook for 1 minute, stirring constantly. Add the chicken to the skillet and cook over medium heat, turning frequently, for 5 minutes, or until the skin has lightly browned, then remove to a plate. Add the onion to the skillet and cook, stirring occasionally, for 10 minutes until soft.

3 Meanwhile, put the stock and saffron into a pan over low heat and heat through.

4 Transfer the chicken and onion to a large casserole dish, add the bell peppers, lemons, and rice, then pour over the stock. Mix well and season with pepper.

5 Cover and cook in a preheated oven, 350°F/180°C, for 50 minutes, or until the chicken is cooked through and tender. Reduce the oven temperature to 325°F/160°C. Add the olives to the casserole and cook for an additional 10 minutes.

6 Serve the dish sprinkled with chopped parsley and accompanied by salad greens.

louisiana chicken

ingredients

serves 4

5 tbsp corn oil
4 chicken parts
6 tbsp all-purpose flour
1 onion, chopped
2 celery stalks, sliced
1 green bell pepper, seeded
 and chopped
2 garlic cloves, finely chopped
2 tsp chopped fresh thyme
2 fresh red chiles, seeded
 and finely chopped
14 oz/400 g canned
 chopped tomatoes
10 fl oz/300 ml/1¼ cups chicken
 stock
salt and pepper
corn salad and chopped
 fresh thyme, to garnish

method

1 Heat the oil in a large, heavy-bottomed pan or flameproof casserole. Add the chicken and cook over medium heat, stirring, for 5–10 minutes, or until golden. Transfer the chicken to a plate with a perforated spoon.

2 Stir the flour into the oil and cook over very low heat, stirring constantly, for 15 minutes, or until light golden. Do not let it burn. Add the onion, celery, and green bell pepper and cook, stirring constantly, for 2 minutes. Add the garlic, thyme, and chiles and cook, stirring, for 1 minute.

3 Stir in the tomatoes and their juices, then gradually stir in the stock. Return the chicken pieces to the pan, cover, and simmer for 45 minutes, or until the chicken is cooked through and tender. Season with salt and pepper, transfer to warmed serving plates and serve immediately, garnished with some corn salad and a sprinkling of chopped thyme.

red hot chili chicken

ingredients

serves 4

1 tbsp curry paste
2 fresh green chiles, chopped
5 dried red chiles
2 tbsp tomato paste
2 garlic cloves, chopped
1 tsp chili powder
pinch of sugar
pinch of salt
2 tbsp peanut or corn oil
½ tsp cumin seeds
1 onion, chopped
2 curry leaves
1 tsp ground cumin
1 tsp ground coriander
½ tsp ground turmeric
14 oz/400 g canned chopped
    tomatoes
5 fl oz/150 ml/⅔ cup chicken stock
4 skinless, boneless chicken breasts
1 tsp garam masala
freshly cooked rice and plain
    yogurt garnished with mint
    sprigs and diced cucumber,
    to serve

method

1 To make the chili paste, place the curry paste, fresh and dried chiles, tomato paste, garlic, chili powder, and sugar in a blender or food processor with the salt. Process to a smooth paste.

2 Heat the oil in a large, heavy-bottom pan. Add the cumin seeds and cook over medium heat, stirring constantly, for 2 minutes, or until they begin to pop and release their aroma. Add the onion and curry leaves and cook, stirring, for 5 minutes.

3 Add the chili paste, cook for 2 minutes, then stir in the ground cumin, coriander, and turmeric and cook for an additional 2 minutes.

4 Add the tomatoes and their juices and the stock. Bring to a boil, then reduce the heat and simmer for 5 minutes. Add the chicken and garam masala, cover, and simmer gently for 20 minutes, or until the chicken is cooked through and tender. Serve immediately with freshly cooked rice and yogurt.

chicken cacciatore

ingredients

serves 4

3 tbsp olive oil
4 lb/1.8 kg skinless chicken parts
red onions, sliced
2 garlic cloves, finely chopped
14 oz/400 g canned chopped
    tomatoes
2 tbsp chopped fresh flat-leaf
    parsley
1 tbsp sun-dried tomato paste
5 fl oz/150 ml/²⁄₃ cup red wine
6 fresh basil leaves
salt and pepper
fresh basil sprigs, to garnish
pasta, to serve

method

1 Heat the olive oil in a flameproof casserole. Add the chicken and cook over medium heat, stirring frequently, for 5–10 minutes, or until golden. Transfer to a plate with a slotted spoon.

2 Add the onions and garlic to the casserole and cook over low heat, stirring occasionally, for 10 minutes, or until golden. Add the tomatoes, the parsley, tomato paste, and wine, and tear in the basil leaves. Season to taste with salt and pepper.

3 Bring the mixture to a boil, then return the chicken to the casserole, pushing it down into the cooking liquid. Cover and cook in a preheated oven, 325°F/160°C, for 1 hour, or until the chicken is cooked through and tender. Garnish with fresh basil sprigs and serve immediately with pasta.

steamed chicken with chile & cilantro butter

ingredients

serves 4

4 tbsp butter, softened
1 fresh Thai chile, seeded
    and chopped
3 tbsp chopped fresh cilantro
4 skinless, boneless chicken
    breasts, about
    6 oz/175 g each
14 fl oz/400 ml/1¾ cups
    coconut milk
12 fl oz/350 ml/1½ cups
    chicken stock
1 cup basmati rice

pickled vegetables

1 carrot
½ cucumber
3 scallions
2 tbsp rice vinegar
salt and pepper

method

1 Mix the butter with the chile and cilantro. Cut a deep slash into the side of each chicken breast to form a pocket. Spoon quarter of the flavoured butter into each pocket and place on a 12-inch/30-cm square of baking parchment.

2 Season to taste with salt and pepper, then bring together 2 opposite sides of the paper on top, folding over to seal firmly. Twist the ends to seal. Pour the coconut milk and stock into a large pan with a steamer top. Bring to a boil.

3 Stir in the rice with a pinch of salt. Put the chicken parcels in the steamer top, cover, and simmer for 15–18 minutes, stirring the rice once, until the rice is tender and the chicken is cooked through. Meanwhile, peel the carrot, then trim the carrot, cucumber, and scallions and cut them into fine sticks. Sprinkle with the vinegar.

4 Unwrap the chicken, reserving the juices, and cut in half diagonally. Serve the chicken on the rice, with the juices spooned over and pickled vegetables on the side.

baked tapenade chicken

ingredients

serves 4

4 skinless, boneless chicken breasts

4 tbsp green olive tapenade

8 thin slices smoked pancetta

2 garlic cloves, coarsely chopped

9 oz/250 g cherry tomatoes,
    halved

4 fl oz/125 ml/scant ½ cup
    dry white wine

2 tbsp olive oil

8 slices ciabatta

salt and pepper

method

1 Put the chicken breasts on a cutting board and cut three deep slashes into each. Spread a tablespoon of the tapenade over each chicken breast, pushing it into the slashes with a palette knife.

2 Wrap each chicken breast in two slices of pancetta. Place the chicken breasts in a shallow ovenproof dish and arrange the garlic and tomatoes around them. Season to taste with salt and pepper, then pour over the wine and 1 tablespoon of the oil.

3 Bake in a preheated oven, 425°F/220°C, for about 20 minutes, until the juices run clear when the chicken is pierced with a skewer. Cover the dish loosely with aluminum foil and let stand for 5 minutes. Meanwhile, preheat the broiler to high.

4 Brush the ciabatta with the remaining oil and cook under the preheated broiler for 2–3 minutes, turning once, until golden.

5 Transfer the chicken and tomatoes to serving plates and spoon over the juices. Serve the dish with the toasted ciabatta.

pistachio chicken korma

ingredients

serves 4

1 lb 9 oz/700 g skinless, boneless chicken breasts or thighs, cut into 1-inch/2.5-cm cubes

1 tsp salt, or to taste

juice of ½ lemon

4 tbsp ghee or unsalted butter

6 green cardamom pods

1 large onion, finely chopped

2 tsp garlic paste

2 tsp ginger paste

1 tbsp ground coriander

½ tsp chili powder

10 oz/280 g/1¼ cups plain yogurt, whisked

good pinch of saffron threads, pounded and soaked in 2 tbsp hot milk

4 oz/115 g/¾ cup shelled pistachios, soaked in 7 fl oz/ 200 ml/scant 1 cup boiling water for 20 minutes

5 fl oz/150 ml/⅔ cup light cream

2 tbsp rose water

6–8 white rose petals, to garnish

cooked basmati rice and lemon wedges, to serve

method

1 Put the chicken in a nonmetallic bowl and add the salt, pepper, and lemon juice. Rub into the chicken, cover, and let marinate in the refrigerator for 30 minutes.

2 Melt the ghee in a medium heavy-bottom saucepan over low heat and add the cardamom pods. When they have puffed up, add the onion and increase the heat to medium. Cook, stirring frequently, until the onion is a pale golden color. Add the garlic paste and ginger paste and cook, stirring frequently, for an additional 2–3 minutes. Add the coriander and chili powder and cook, stirring, for 30 seconds. Add the chicken, increase the heat to medium–high, and cook, stirring continuously, for 5–6 minutes, until it changes color.

3 Reduce the heat to low and add the yogurt and the saffron-and-milk mixture. Bring to a slow simmer, cover, and cook for 15 minutes. Stir halfway through to ensure that it does not stick to the bottom of the pan.

4 Meanwhile, put the pistachios and their soaking water in a blender or food processor and process until smooth. Add to the chicken mixture, followed by the cream. Cover and simmer, stirring occasionally, for an additional 15–20 minutes. Stir in the rose water and remove from the heat. Garnish with the rose petals and serve with cooked basmati rice and lemon wedges.

chicken with walnut sauce

ingredients

serves 4

4–8 skinless chicken parts
½ lemon, cut into wedges
3 tbsp olive oil
5 fl oz/150 ml/⅔ cup dry
    white wine
10 fl oz/300 ml/1¼ cups
    chicken stock
1 bay leaf
3½ oz/100 g/¾ cup walnut pieces
2 garlic cloves
5 fl oz/150 ml/⅔ cup strained
    plain yogurt
salt and pepper
chopped fresh flat-leaf parsley,
    to garnish
rice or pilaf and pita bread,
    to serve

method

1 Rub the chicken parts with the lemon. Heat the oil in a large skillet, add the chicken pieces, and fry quickly until lightly browned on all sides.

2 Pour the wine into the skillet and bring to a boil. Add the stock, bay leaf, salt, and pepper and simmer for about 20 minutes, turning several times, until the chicken is tender.

3 Meanwhile, put the walnuts and garlic in a food processor and blend to form a fairly smooth purée.

4 When the chicken is cooked, transfer to a warmed serving dish and keep warm. Stir the walnut mixture and yogurt into the pan juices and heat gently for about 5 minutes until the sauce is quite thick. (Do not boil or the sauce will curdle.) Season with salt and pepper.

5 Pour the walnut sauce over the chicken pieces and serve hot with rice, or pilaf, and pita bread. Garnish with chopped fresh parsley.

chicken kiev

ingredients

serves 4

4 tbsp butter, softened
1 garlic clove, finely chopped
1 tbsp finely chopped fresh parsley
1 tbsp finely chopped fresh
    oregano
4 skinless, boneless chicken breasts
3 oz/85 g fresh white or
    whole wheat bread crumbs
3 tbsp freshly grated Parmesan
    cheese
1 egg, beaten
9 fl oz/250 ml vegetable oil,
    for deep-frying
salt and pepper
slices of lemon and flat-leaf parsley
    sprigs, to garnish
freshly cooked new potatoes and
    selection of cooked vegetables,
    to serve

method

1 Place the butter and garlic in a bowl and mix together well. Stir in the chopped herbs and season well with salt and pepper. Pound the chicken breasts to flatten them to an even thickness, then place a tablespoon of herb butter in the center of each one. Fold in the sides to enclose the butter, then secure with wooden toothpicks.

2 Combine the bread crumbs and grated Parmesan on a plate. Dip the chicken parcels into the beaten egg, then coat in the bread crumb mixture. Transfer to a plate, cover, and let chill for 30 minutes. Remove from the refrigerator and coat in the egg and then the breadcrumb mixture for a second time.

3 Pour the oil into a deep-fryer to a depth that will cover the chicken parcels. Heat until it reaches 350–375°F/ 180–190°C, or until a cube of bread browns in 30 seconds. Transfer the chicken to the hot oil and deep-fry for 5 minutes, or until cooked through. Lift out the chicken and drain on paper towels.

4 Divide the chicken among 4 serving plates, garnish with lemon slices and parsley sprigs, and serve with new potatoes and a selection of vegetables.

chicken fricassée

ingredients

serves 4

1 tbsp all-purpose flour
salt and white pepper
4 skinless, boneless chicken
    breasts, about 5 oz/140 g each,
    trimmed of all visible fat and
    cut into ¾-inch/2-cm cubes
1 tbsp sunflower or corn oil
8 pearl onions
2 garlic cloves, crushed
8 fl oz/250 ml/1 cup chicken stock
2 carrots, diced
2 celery stalks, diced
8 oz/225 g/2 cups frozen peas
1 yellow bell pepper, seeded
    and diced
4 oz/115 g white mushrooms,
    sliced
4 fl oz/125 ml/½ cup lowfat plain
    yogurt
3 tbsp chopped fresh parsley

method

1 Spread out the flour on a dish and season with salt and pepper. Add the chicken and, using your hands, coat in the flour. Heat the oil in a heavy-bottom pan. Add the onions and garlic and cook over low heat, stirring occasionally, for 5 minutes. Add the chicken and cook, stirring, for 10 minutes, or until just beginning to color.

2 Gradually stir in the stock, then add the carrots, celery, and peas. Bring to a boil, then reduce the heat, cover, and let simmer for 5 minutes. Add the bell pepper and mushrooms, cover, and let simmer for an additional 10 minutes.

3 Stir in the yogurt and chopped parsley and season with salt and pepper. Cook for 1–2 minutes, or until heated through, then transfer to 4 large, warmed serving plates and serve immediately.

noodles
& pasta

noodle basket with chicken-lime salad

ingredients

serves 4

peanut or corn oil, for
    deep-frying and oiling
9 oz/250 g fresh thin or medium
    Chinese egg noodles

chicken-lime salad
6 tbsp mayonnaise
6 tbsp sour cream
1-inch/2.5-cm piece fresh ginger,
    peeled and grated
grated rind and juice of 1 lime
4 skinless, boneless chicken thighs,
    poached and cooled, then cut
    into thin strips
1 carrot, peeled and grated
1 cucumber, cut in half lengthwise,
    seeded and sliced
1 tbsp finely chopped fresh cilantro
1 tbsp finely chopped fresh mint
1 tbsp finely chopped fresh parsley
several fresh basil leaves, torn
salt and pepper

method

1 To shape noodle baskets, you will need a special set of 2 long-handled wire baskets that clip inside each other, available from gourmet kitchen stores. Dip the larger wire basket in oil, then line it completely and evenly with one-fourth of the tangled noodles. Dip the smaller wire basket in oil, then position it inside the larger basket and clip it into position.

2 Heat 4 inches/10 cm of oil in a wok or deep-fat fryer to 350–375°F/180–190°C, or until a cube of bread browns in 30 seconds. Lower the baskets into the oil and deep-fry for 2–3 minutes, or until the noodles are golden brown. Remove the baskets from the oil and drain on paper towels. Unclip the 2 wire baskets and carefully remove the small one. Use a round-bladed knife, if necessary, to prise the noodle basket from the wire frame. Repeat to make 3 more baskets. Let the noodle baskets cool.

3 To make the salad, combine the mayonnaise, sour cream, ginger, and lime rind. Gradually add the lime juice until you get the flavor you like. Stir in the chicken, carrot, cucumber, salt, and pepper. Cover and let chill. Just before serving, stir in the herbs and spoon the salad into the noodle baskets.

yaki soba

ingredients

serves 2

14 oz/400 g ramen noodles
1 onion, finely sliced
7 oz/200 g fresh bean sprouts
1 red bell pepper, seeded and
thinly sliced
1 boneless, skin-on cooked
chicken breast, about
5½ oz/150 g, sliced
12 cooked, shelled shrimp
1 tbsp peanut oil
2 tbsp shoyu (Japanese soy sauce)
½ tbsp mirin
1 tsp sesame oil
1 tsp toasted sesame seeds
2 scallions, finely sliced

method

1 Cook the noodles according to the package instructions. Drain well and tip into a bowl.

2 Mix the onion, bean sprouts, bell pepper, chicken, and shrimp together in a separate bowl. Stir through the noodles.

3 Heat a wok over a high heat, then add the peanut oil. Add the noodle mixture and stir-fry for 4 minutes, or until golden, then add the shoyu, mirin, and sesame oil and toss together.

4 Divide the mixture between 2 plates, sprinkle with the sesame seeds and scallions, and serve immediately.

teriyaki chicken with sesame noodles

ingredients

serves 4

4 boneless chicken breasts, about
    6 oz/175 g each, with or
    without skin, as you wish
about 4 tbsp bottled teriyaki sauce
peanut or corn oil
cucumber fans, to garnish

sesame noodles

9 oz/250 g dried thin buckwheat
    noodles
1 tbsp toasted sesame oil
2 tbsp toasted sesame seeds
2 tbsp finely chopped fresh parsley
salt and pepper

method

1 Using a sharp knife, score each chicken breast diagonally across 3 times and rub all over with teriyaki sauce. Set aside to marinate for at least 10 minutes.

2 When you are ready to cook the chicken, preheat the broiler to high. Bring a pan of water to a boil, add the buckwheat noodles, and boil for 3 minutes, or according to the package instructions, until soft. Drain and rinse well in cold water to stop the cooking and remove excess starch, then drain again.

3 Lightly brush the broiler rack with oil. Add the chicken breasts, skin-side up, and brush again with a little extra teriyaki sauce. Broil the chicken breasts about 4 inches/ 10 cm from the heat, brushing occasionally with extra teriyaki sauce, for 15 minutes, or until cooked through and the juices run clear.

4 Meanwhile, heat a wok or large skillet over high heat. Add the sesame oil and heat until it shimmers. Add the noodles and stir around to heat through, then stir in the sesame seeds and parsley. Season with salt and pepper. To serve, transfer the chicken breasts to plates and add a portion of noodles to each. Garnish with cucumber fans.

chicken chow mein

ingredients

serves 4

9 oz/250 g packet medium
    egg noodles

2 tbsp sunflower oil

10 oz/280 g cooked chicken
    breasts, shredded

1 garlic clove, finely chopped

1 red bell pepper, seeded
    and thinly sliced

3½ oz/100 g shiitake
    mushrooms, sliced

6 scallions, sliced

3½ oz/100 g bean sprouts

3 tbsp soy sauce

1 tbsp sesame oil

method

1 Place the egg noodles in a large bowl or dish and break them up slightly. Pour enough boiling water over the noodles to cover and let stand while preparing the other ingredients.

2 Preheat a wok over medium heat. Add the sunflower oil and swirl it around to coat the sides of the wok. When the oil is hot, add the shredded chicken, garlic, bell pepper, mushrooms, scallions, and bean sprouts to the wok and stir-fry for about 5 minutes.

3 Drain the noodles thoroughly then add them to the wok, toss well, and stir-fry for an additional 5 minutes. Drizzle the soy sauce and sesame oil over the chow mein and toss until well combined.

4 Transfer the chicken chow mein to warmed serving bowls and serve immediately.

variation

Add 1 teaspoon of Chinese five spice to the pan just before you add the chicken and stir for a few seconds to release the aromas.

chicken & green vegetables

ingredients

serves 4

9 oz/250 g dried medium Chinese
   egg noodles

2 tbsp peanut or corn oil

1 large garlic clove, crushed

1 fresh green chile, seeded
   and sliced

1 tbsp Chinese five-spice powder

2 skinless, boneless chicken
   breasts, cut into thin strips

2 green bell peppers, cored,
   seeded, and sliced

4 oz/115 g broccoli, cut into
   small florets

2 oz/55 g green beans, trimmed
   and cut into
    1½-inch/4-cm pieces

5 tbsp vegetable or chicken stock

2 tbsp bottled oyster sauce

2 tbsp soy sauce

1 tbsp rice wine or dry sherry

2 oz/55 g/⅔ cup bean sprouts

method

1 Cook the noodles in a pan of boiling water for 4 minutes, or according to the package instructions, until soft. Drain, rinse, and drain again, then set aside.

2 Heat a wok or large skillet over high heat. Add 1 tablespoon of the oil and heat until it shimmers. Add the garlic, chile, and five-spice powder and stir-fry for about 30 seconds.

3 Add the chicken and stir-fry for 3 minutes, or until it is cooked through. Use a slotted spoon to remove the chicken from the wok and set aside.

4 Add the remaining oil to the wok and heat until it shimmers. Add the bell peppers, broccoli, and beans and stir-fry for about 2 minutes. Stir in the stock, oyster sauce, soy sauce, and rice wine and return the chicken to the wok. Continue stir-frying for about 1 minute, until the chicken is reheated and the vegetables are tender, but still firm to the bite. Add the noodles and bean sprouts and use 2 forks to mix all the ingredients together.

pappardelle with chicken & porcini

ingredients

serves 4

1½ oz/40 g dried porcini
    mushrooms
6 fl oz/175 ml/¾ cup hot water
1 lb 12 oz/800 g canned
    chopped tomatoes
1 fresh red chile, seeded and
    finely chopped
3 tbsp olive oil
12 oz/350 g skinless, boneless
    chicken, cut into thin strips
2 garlic cloves, finely chopped
12 oz/350 g dried pappardelle
salt and pepper
2 tbsp chopped fresh flat-leaf
    parsley, to garnish

method

1 Place the porcini in a small bowl, add the hot water, and let soak for 30 minutes. Meanwhile, place the tomatoes and their can juices in a heavy-bottom pan and break them up with a wooden spoon, then stir in the chile. Bring to a boil, then reduce the heat and let simmer, stirring occasionally, for 30 minutes.

2 Remove the mushrooms with a slotted spoon, reserving the liquid. Strain the liquid into the tomatoes through a coffee filter paper, or a strainer lined with cheesecloth, and let simmer for 15 minutes.

3 Meanwhile, heat 2 tablespoons of the olive oil in a heavy-bottom skillet. Add the chicken and cook, stirring frequently, until golden brown all over and tender. Stir in the mushrooms and garlic and cook for an additional 5 minutes.

4 While the chicken is cooking, bring a large, heavy-bottom pan of lightly salted water to a boil. Add the pasta, return to a boil, and cook for 8–10 minutes, or until tender but still firm to the bite. Drain well, then transfer to a warmed serving dish. Drizzle with the remaining olive oil and toss lightly. Stir the chicken mixture into the tomato sauce, season, and spoon onto the pasta. Toss lightly, sprinkle with parsley, and serve at once.

spaghetti with parsley chicken

ingredients

serves 4

1 tbsp olive oil
thinly pared rind of 1 lemon,
    cut into julienne strips
1 tsp finely chopped fresh ginger
1 tsp sugar
salt
8 fl oz/250 ml/1 cup chicken stock
9 oz/250 g dried spaghetti
4 tbsp butter
8 oz/225 g skinless, boneless
    chicken breasts, diced
1 red onion, finely chopped
leaves from 2 bunches of
    flat-leaf parsley

method

1 Heat the olive oil in a heavy-bottom pan. Add the lemon rind and cook over low heat, stirring frequently, for 5 minutes. Stir in the ginger and sugar, season with salt, and cook, stirring constantly, for an additional 2 minutes. Pour in the chicken stock, bring to a boil, then cook for 5 minutes, or until the liquid has reduced by half.

2 Meanwhile, bring a large heavy-bottom pan of lightly salted water to a boil. Add the pasta, return to a boil, and cook for 8–10 minutes, or until tender but still firm to the bite.

3 Meanwhile, melt half the butter in a skillet. Add the chicken and onion and cook, stirring frequently, for 5 minutes, or until the chicken is light brown all over. Stir in the lemon and ginger mixture and cook for 1 minute. Stir in the parsley leaves and cook, stirring constantly, for an additional 3 minutes.

4 Drain the pasta and transfer to a warmed serving dish, then add the remaining butter and toss well. Add the chicken sauce, toss again, and serve.

pasta with chicken & feta

ingredients

serves 4

2 tbsp olive oil

1 lb/450 g skinless, boneless chicken breasts, cut into thin strips

6 scallions, chopped

8 oz/225 g Feta cheese, diced

4 tbsp chopped fresh chives

1 lb/450 g dried garganelli

salt and pepper

tomato focaccia, to serve

method

1 Heat the olive oil in a heavy-bottom skillet. Add the chicken and cook over medium heat, stirring frequently, for 5–8 minutes, or until golden all over and cooked through. Add the scallions and cook for 2 minutes. Stir the Feta cheese into the skillet with half the chives and season with salt and pepper.

2 Meanwhile, bring a large heavy-bottom pan of lightly salted water to a boil. Add the pasta, return to a boil, and cook for 8–10 minutes, or until tender but still firm to the bite. Drain well, then transfer to a warmed serving dish.

3 Spoon the chicken mixture onto the pasta, toss lightly, and serve immediately, garnished with the remaining chives and accompanied by tomato focaccia.

chicken with creamy penne

ingredients

serves 2

7 oz/200 g dried penne
1 tbsp olive oil
2 skinless, boneless chicken
   breasts
4 tbsp dry white wine
4 oz/115 g/¾ cup frozen peas
5 tbsp heavy cream
salt
4–5 tbsp chopped fresh
   parsley, to garnish

method

1 Bring a large saucepan of lightly salted water to a boil. Add the pasta, bring back to a boil, and cook for about 8–10 minutes, or according to the package directions, until tender but still firm to the bite.

2 Meanwhile, heat the oil in a skillet, add the chicken, and cook over medium heat for about 4 minutes on each side.

3 Pour in the wine and cook over high heat until it has almost evaporated. Drain the pasta. Add the peas, cream, and pasta to the skillet and stir well. Cover and simmer for 2 minutes. Garnish with fresh parsley and serve.

chicken with linguine & artichokes

ingredients

serves 4

4 skinless, boneless chicken breasts
finely grated rind and juice of
    1 lemon
2 tbsp olive oil
2 garlic cloves, crushed
14 oz/400 g canned artichoke
    hearts, drained and sliced
9 oz/250 g baby plum tomatoes
10½ oz/300 g dried linguine
chopped fresh parsley and finely
    grated Parmesan cheese,
    to garnish

method

1 Put each chicken breast in turn between 2 pieces of plastic wrap and bash with a rolling pin to flatten. Put the chicken into a shallow, nonmetallic dish with the lemon rind and juice and 1 tablespoon of the oil and turn to coat in the marinade. Cover and let marinate in the refrigerator for 30 minutes.

2 Heat the remaining oil in a skillet over low heat, add the garlic, and cook for 1 minute, stirring frequently. Add the artichokes and tomatoes and cook for 5 minutes, stirring occasionally. Add about half the marinade from the chicken and cook over medium heat for an additional 5 minutes.

3 Preheat the broiler to high. Remove the chicken from the remaining marinade and arrange on the broiler pan. Cook the chicken under the preheated broiler for 5 minutes each side until thoroughly cooked through. Meanwhile, add the linguine to a pan of boiling water and cook for 7–9 minutes, or until just tender.

4 Drain the pasta and return to the pan, pour over the artichoke and tomato mixture, and slice in the cooked chicken. Divide among 4 warmed plates and sprinkle over the parsley and cheese.

chicken lasagna

ingredients

serves 6

2 tbsp olive oil
2 lb/900 g/4 cups fresh
    ground chicken
1 garlic clove, finely chopped
4 carrots, chopped
4 leeks, sliced
16 fl oz/500 ml/2 cups
    chicken stock
2 tbsp tomato paste
4 oz/115 g Cheddar cheese, grated
1 tsp Dijon mustard
béchamel sauce (see below)
4 oz/115 g dried lasagna
salt and pepper

béchamel sauce

20 fl oz/625 ml/2½ cups milk
1 bay leaf
6 black peppercorns
2 slices of onion
mace blade
4 tbsp butter
6 tbsp all-purpose flour
salt and pepper
wild arugula and Parmesan
    shavings, to serve

method

1 To make the béchamel sauce, pour the milk into a pan and add the bay leaf, peppercorns, onion, and mace. Heat gently to just below boiling point, then remove from the heat, cover, let infuse for 10 minutes, then strain. Melt the butter in a separate pan. Sprinkle in the flour and cook over low heat, stirring continuously, for 1 minute. Gradually stir in the milk, then bring to a boil and cook, stirring, until thickened and smooth. Season.

2 Heat the oil in a heavy-bottom pan. Add the chicken and cook over medium heat, breaking it up with a wooden spoon, for 5 minutes, or until browned all over. Add the garlic, carrots, and leeks, and cook, stirring occasionally, for 5 minutes.

3 Stir in the chicken stock and tomato paste and season with salt and pepper. Bring to a boil, reduce the heat, cover, and let simmer for 30 minutes.

4 Whisk half the Cheddar cheese and the mustard into the hot béchamel sauce. In a large ovenproof dish, make alternate layers of the chicken mixture, lasagna, and cheese sauce, ending with a layer of cheese sauce. Sprinkle with the remaining Cheddar cheese and bake in a preheated oven, 375°F/190°C, for 1 hour, or until golden brown and bubbling. Serve immediately, with arugula and Parmesan shavings.

chicken & wild mushroom cannelloni

ingredients

serves 4

2 tbsp olive oil

2 garlic cloves, crushed

1 large onion, finely chopped

8 oz/225 g wild mushrooms, sliced

12 oz/350 g ground chicken

4 oz/115 g prosciutto, diced

5 fl oz/150 ml/⅔ cup Marsala wine

7 oz/200 g canned chopped
    tomatoes

1 tbsp shredded fresh basil leaves

2 tbsp tomato paste

10–12 dried cannelloni tubes

butter, for greasing

20 fl oz/625 ml/2½ cups béchamel
    sauce (see page 170)

3 oz/85 g/¾ cup freshly grated
    Parmesan cheese

salt and pepper

method

1 Heat the olive oil in a heavy-bottom skillet. Add the garlic, onion, and mushrooms and cook over low heat, stirring frequently, for 8–10 minutes. Add the ground chicken and prosciutto and cook, stirring frequently, for 12 minutes, or until browned all over. Stir in the Marsala, tomatoes and their can juices, basil, and tomato paste and cook for 4 minutes. Season with salt and pepper, then cover and let simmer for 30 minutes. Uncover, stir, and let simmer for 15 minutes.

2 Meanwhile, bring a large, heavy-bottom pan of lightly salted water to a boil. Add the pasta, return to a boil, and cook for 8–10 minutes, or until tender but still firm to the bite. Using a slotted spoon, transfer the pasta to a plate and pat dry with paper towels.

3 Using a teaspoon, fill the cannelloni tubes with the chicken, prosciutto, and mushroom mixture. Transfer them to a large, lightly greased ovenproof dish. Pour the béchamel sauce over them to cover completely and sprinkle with the grated Parmesan cheese.

4 Bake the cannelloni in a preheated oven, 375°F/190°C, for 30 minutes, or until golden brown and bubbling. Serve immediately.

rice

chicken fried rice

ingredients

serves 4

½ tbsp sesame oil
6 shallots, peeled and cut
    into quarters
3 cups cubed cooked chicken
3 tbsp soy sauce
2 carrots, diced
1 celery stalk, diced
1 red bell pepper, seeded and diced
6 oz/175 g/1¼ cups fresh peas
3½ oz/100 g/⅔ cup drained
    canned corn kernels
9¾ oz/275 g/1¾ cups cooked
    long-grain rice
2 large eggs

method

1 Heat a wok or large skillet over a medium heat, add the oil, and heat it.

2 Add the shallots and fry until soft, then add the chicken and 2 tablespoons of the soy sauce and stir-fry for 5–6 minutes.

3 Stir in the carrots, celery, red bell pepper, peas, and corn and stir-fry for an additional 5 minutes. Add the rice and stir thoroughly. Beat the eggs and pour into the mixture. Stir until the eggs are beginning to set, then add in the remaining soy sauce. Transfer to bowls and serve immediately.

risotto with chargrilled chicken breast

ingredients

serves 4

4 boneless chicken breasts,
  about 4 oz/115 g each
grated rind and juice of 1 lemon
5 tbsp olive oil
1 garlic clove, crushed
8 fresh thyme sprigs, finely
  chopped
3 tbsp butter
1 small onion, finely chopped
10 oz/280 g/1½ cups risotto rice
5 fl oz/150 ml/²/₃ cup dry white
  wine
32 fl oz/1 liter/4 cups simmering
  chicken stock
3 oz/85 g/¾ cup freshly grated
  Parmesan or Grana Padano
  cheese
salt and pepper
lemon wedges and fresh thyme
  sprigs, to garnish

method

1 Place the chicken breasts in a shallow, nonmetallic dish and season. Mix together the lemon rind and juice, 4 tablespoons of the olive oil, the garlic, and thyme. Spoon over the chicken and rub in. Cover and marinate for 4–6 hours, then return to room temperature.

2 Preheat a grill pan over high heat. Cook the chicken, skin-side down, for 10 minutes, or until the skin is crisp and starting to brown. Turn over and brown the underside. Reduce the heat and cook for 10–15 minutes, or until the juices run clear. Let rest on a carving board for 5 minutes, then cut into thick slices.

3 Meanwhile, melt 2 tablespoons of the butter with the remaining oil in a pan over medium heat. Cook the onion, stirring occasionally, until soft and starting to turn golden. Reduce the heat, stir in the rice, and cook, stirring, for 2–3 minutes, until translucent. Add the wine and cook, stirring, for 1 minute until reduced. Add the hot stock, a ladleful at a time, stirring constantly, until all the liquid is absorbed and the rice is creamy. Season with salt and pepper. Remove from the heat and stir in the remaining butter, then melt in the cheese. Serve at once, topped with the chicken slices and garnished with lemon wedges and thyme sprigs.

chicken, mushroom & cashew nut risotto

ingredients

serves 4

2 oz/55 g butter

1 onion, chopped

9 oz/250 g skinless, boneless chicken breasts, diced

12 oz/350 g/1¾ cups risotto rice

1 tsp ground turmeric

5 fl oz/150 ml/⅔ cup white wine

46 fl oz/1.4 liters/generous 5½ cups simmering chicken stock

2¾ oz/75 g cremini mushrooms, sliced

1¾ oz/50 g/scant ⅓ cup cashew nuts, halved

salt and pepper

wild arugula, fresh Parmesan cheese shavings, and fresh basil leaves, to garnish

method

1 Melt the butter in a large pan over medium heat. Add the onion and cook, stirring occasionally, for 5 minutes, or until softened. Add the chicken and cook, stirring frequently, for an additional 5 minutes. Reduce the heat, add the rice, and mix to coat in butter. Cook, stirring constantly, for 2–3 minutes, or until the grains are translucent. Stir in the turmeric, then add the wine. Cook, stirring continuously, for 1 minute until reduced.

2 Gradually add the hot stock, a ladleful at a time. Stir constantly and add more liquid as the rice absorbs each addition. Increase the heat to medium so that the liquid bubbles. Cook for 20 minutes, or until all the liquid is absorbed and the rice is creamy. About 3 minutes before the end of the cooking time, stir in the mushrooms and cashews. Season with salt and pepper.

3 Arrange the arugula leaves on 4 individual serving plates. Remove the risotto from the heat and spoon it over the arugula. Sprinkle over the Parmesan shavings and basil leaves and serve.

risotto alla milanese

ingredients

serves 4

4½ oz/125 g butter
2 lb/900 g skinless, boneless
   chicken breasts, thinly sliced
1 large onion, chopped
1 lb 2 oz/500 g risotto rice
5 fl oz/150 ml white wine
1 tsp crushed saffron threads
20 fl oz/625 ml/2½ cups
   simmering chicken stock
salt and pepper
fresh flat-leaf parsley sprigs,
   to garnish
2 oz/55 g Parmesan cheese
   shavings, to serve

method

1 Melt 2 oz/55 g of the butter in a deep skillet. Add the chicken and onion and cook over medium heat, stirring occasionally, for 8–10 minutes, until golden brown.

2 Reduce the heat, add the rice and cook, stirring constantly, for a few minutes until the grains begin to swell and are thoroughly coated in the butter.

3 Add the wine and saffron and season with salt and pepper. Cook, stirring continuously, until the wine has completely evaporated. Add 2 ladlefuls of the hot stock and cook, stirring continuously, until it has been completely absorbed. Add the remaining stock, 1 ladleful at a time, stirring continuously and allowing each ladleful to be absorbed before adding the next, until all the stock has been absorbed and the rice has a creamy texture—this will take 20–25 minutes.

4 Garnish each individual plate with a parsley sprig, then serve the risotto immediately, sprinkled with the Parmesan cheese shavings and dotted with the remaining butter.

chicken basquaise

ingredients

serves 4–5

3 lb/1.3 kg chicken, cut into
   8 parts
flour, for coating
3 tbsp olive oil
1 Bermuda onion, thickly sliced
2 red, green, or yellow bell
   peppers, seeded and cut
   lengthwise into thick strips
2 garlic cloves
5 oz/150 g chorizo sausage,
   skinned and cut into 1/2-inch/
   1-cm pieces
1 tbsp tomato paste
7 oz/200 g/1 cup long-grain
   white rice
16 fl oz/450 ml/2 cups chicken
   stock
1 tsp crushed dried chiles
1/2 tsp dried thyme
4 oz/115 g Bayonne or other
   air-dried ham, diced
12 dry-cured black olives
2 tbsp chopped fresh parsley
salt and pepper

method

1 Pat the chicken parts dry with paper towels. Put 2 tablespoons of flour in a plastic bag, season well with salt and pepper, and add the chicken parts. Seal the bag and shake to coat the chicken. Heat 2 tablespoons of the oil in a large flameproof casserole over medium–high heat. Add the chicken and cook, turning frequently, for 15 minutes, or until well browned all over. Transfer to a plate.

2 Heat the remaining oil in the casserole and add the onion and bell peppers. Reduce the heat to medium and stir-fry until beginning to color and soften. Add the garlic, chorizo, and tomato paste and cook, stirring continuously, for about 3 minutes. Add the rice and cook, stirring to coat, for 2 minutes, or until the rice is translucent. Add the stock, crushed chiles, and thyme, season to taste with salt and pepper, and stir well.

3 Bring to a boil. Return the chicken to the casserole, pressing it gently into the rice. Cover and cook over a very low heat for 45 minutes, or until the chicken is cooked through and the rice is tender. Stir the ham, black olives, and half the parsley into the rice mixture.

4 Re-cover and heat through for another 5 minutes. Sprinkle with the remaining parsley and serve the casserole immediately.

chicken & shrimp paella

ingredients

serves 6–8

½ tsp saffron threads
2 tbsp hot water
about 6 tbsp olive oil
6–8 chicken thighs, (on the bone,
    skin on), excess fat removed
5 oz/140 g Spanish chorizo
    sausage, casing removed,
    cut into ¼-inch/5-mm slices
2 large onions, chopped
4 large garlic cloves, crushed
1 tsp mild or hot Spanish paprika
13 oz/375 g/generous 1½ cups
    medium-grain paella rice
3½ oz/100 g green beans, chopped
3 oz/85 g/¾ cup frozen peas
40 fl oz/1.25 liters/5 cups
    chicken stock
16 live mussels, scrubbed and
    debearded (discard any that
    do not shut when tapped)
16 raw shrimp, shelled, and
    deveined
2 red bell peppers, broiled,
    peeled, seeded, and sliced
salt and pepper
1¼ oz/35 g fresh parsley, chopped,
    to garnish

method

1 Put the saffron threads and water in a small bowl and let infuse for a few minutes.

2 Heat 3 tablespoons of the oil in a 12-inch/30-cm paella pan. Cook the chicken thighs over medium-high heat, turning frequently, for 5 minutes, or until golden and crispy. Transfer to a bowl. Add the chorizo to the pan and cook, stirring, for 1 minute, or until beginning to crisp. Add to the chicken.

3 Heat another 3 tablespoons of the oil in the pan and cook the onions, stirring frequently, for 2 minutes, then add the garlic and paprika and cook, stirring, for 3 minutes, or until the onions are soft, but not browned. Add the rice, beans, and peas and stir until coated in oil. Return the chicken, chorizo, and any juices to the pan. Stir in the stock and the saffron with its soaking liquid, and season with salt and pepper. Bring to a boil, stirring continuously, then let simmer, uncovered, for 15 minutes, or until the rice is almost tender and most of the liquid has been absorbed.

4 Arrange the mussels, shrimp, and red bell pepper slices on top, then cover and let simmer, without stirring, for 5 minutes, or until the shrimp turn pink and the mussels open. Discard any mussels that remain closed. Serve immediately, sprinkled with the parsley.

sunshine paella

ingredients

serves 4–6

½ tsp saffron threads

2 tbsp hot water

5½ oz/150 g cod, rinsed

46 fl oz/1.4 liters/5½ cups
   simmering fish stock

12 large raw shrimp, shelled
   and deveined

7 oz/200 g live mussels,
   scrubbed and debearded

3 tbsp olive oil

5½ oz/150 g chicken breast,
   cut into bite-size chunks

1 large red onion, chopped

2 garlic cloves, chopped

½ tsp cayenne pepper

½ tsp paprika

8 oz/225 g tomatoes, peeled
   and cut into wedges

1 red bell pepper and 1 yellow bell
   pepper, seeded and sliced

12 oz/350 g/1½ cups paella rice

salt and pepper

6 oz/175 g/scant 1 cup canned
   corn kernels, drained

3 hard-cooked eggs, cut into
   fourths lengthwise, to serve

lemon wedges, to serve

method

1 Put the saffron threads and water in a bowl and let infuse. Cook the cod in the simmering stock for 5 minutes. Rinse, drain, cut into chunks, and set aside in a bowl. Cook the shrimp in the stock for 2 minutes. Add to the cod. Discard any mussels with broken shells or that refuse to close when tapped. Add to the stock and cook until opened. Add to the bowl with the other seafood, discarding any that remain closed.

2 Heat the oil in a paella pan over medium heat. Cook the chicken, stirring, for 5 minutes. Add the onion and cook, stirring, until softened. Add the garlic, cayenne pepper, paprika, and saffron and its soaking liquid and cook, stirring, for 1 minute. Add the tomatoes and bell peppers and cook, stirring, for 2 minutes.

3 Add the rice and cook, stirring, for 1 minute. Add most of the stock, bring to a boil, then let simmer, uncovered, for 10 minutes. Do not stir during cooking, but shake the pan once or twice and when adding ingredients. Season, then cook for 10 minutes, or until the rice is almost cooked, adding more stock if necessary. Add the seafood and corn and cook for 3 minutes.

4 When all the liquid has been absorbed, remove from the heat. Cover and let stand for 5 minutes. Serve topped with egg fourths and garnished with lemon wedges.

chicken & duck paella with orange

ingredients

serves 4–6

½ tsp saffron threads

2 tbsp hot water

6 oz/175 g skinless, boneless
chicken breast

4 large skinless, boneless
duck breasts

2 tbsp olive oil

1 large onion, chopped

2 garlic cloves, crushed

1 tsp paprika

8 oz/225 g tomato wedges

1 orange bell pepper, broiled,
peeled, seeded and chopped

6 oz/175 g canned red kidney
beans (drained weight)

12 oz/350 g/1½ cups paella rice

1 tbsp chopped fresh flat-leaf
parsley, plus extra sprigs
to garnish

1 tbsp freshly grated orange rind

2 tbsp orange juice

3½ fl oz/100 ml/generous
⅓ cup white wine

40 fl oz/1.25 liters/5 cups
simmering chicken stock

salt and pepper

orange wedges, to garnish

method

1 Put the saffron threads and water in a small bowl and let infuse for a few minutes.

2 Cut the chicken and duck into bite-size chunks and season. Heat the oil in a paella pan and cook the chicken and duck over medium-high heat, stirring, until golden all over. Transfer to a bowl and set aside.

3 Add the onion and cook over medium heat, stirring, until softened. Add the garlic, paprika, and saffron and its soaking liquid and cook, stirring continuously, for 1 minute. Add the tomato wedges, orange bell pepper, and beans and cook, stirring, for an additional 2 minutes.

4 Add the rice and parsley and cook, stirring, for 1 minute. Add the orange rind and juice, the wine, and most of the hot stock. Bring to a boil, then let simmer, uncovered, for 10 minutes. Do not stir during cooking, but shake the pan once or twice, and when adding ingredients. Return the chicken and duck to the pan and season. Cook for 10–15 minutes, or until the rice grains are plump and cooked, adding a little more stock if necessary.

5 When all the liquid has been absorbed and you detect a faint toasty aroma coming from the rice, remove from the heat. Cover with foil and let stand for 5 minutes. Garnish with parsley sprigs and orange wedges to serve.

paella with pork & chorizo

ingredients

serves 4–6

12 large raw shrimp, in their shells

2 pints/1.25 liters/5 cups
simmering fish stock

½ tsp saffron threads

2 tbsp hot water

3½ oz/100 g skinless, boneless
chicken breast, cut into
½-inch/1-cm pieces

3½ oz/100 g pork tenderloin,
cut into ½-inch/1-cm pieces

3 tbsp olive oil

3½ oz/100 g Spanish chorizo
sausage, casing removed,
cut into ½-inch/1-cm slices

1 large red onion, chopped

2 garlic cloves, crushed

½ tsp cayenne pepper

½ tsp paprika

1 red bell pepper, seeded
and sliced

1 green bell pepper, seeded
and sliced

12 cherry tomatoes, halved

12 oz/350 g/1½ cups paella rice

1 tbsp chopped fresh parsley

2 tsp chopped fresh tarragon

salt and pepper

method

1 Add the shrimp to the simmering stock and cook for
2 minutes, then transfer to a bowl and set aside. Put the
saffron threads and water in a small bowl and let infuse.

2 Season the chicken and pork with salt and pepper.
Heat the oil in a paella pan and cook the chicken, pork,
and chorizo over medium heat, stirring, until golden.
Add the onion and cook, stirring, until softened. Add
the garlic, cayenne pepper, paprika, and saffron and
its soaking liquid and cook, stirring continuously, for
1 minute. Add the bell pepper slices and tomato halves
and cook, stirring, for an additional 2 minutes.

3 Add the rice and herbs and cook, stirring continuously,
for 1 minute. Pour in most of the hot stock, bring to a
boil, then let simmer, uncovered, for 10 minutes. Do
not stir during cooking, but shake the pan once or
twice and when adding ingredients. Season, then cook
for an additional 10 minutes, or until the rice is almost
cooked, adding a little more hot stock if necessary.
Add the shrimp and cook for an additional 2 minutes.

4 When all the liquid has been absorbed and you
detect a faint toasty aroma coming from the rice,
remove from the heat. Cover with foil and let stand
for 5 minutes. Serve.

greek chicken with rice

ingredients

serves 4

8 chicken thighs
2 tbsp corn oil
1 onion, chopped
2 garlic cloves, finely chopped
6 oz/175 g/scant 1 cup
   long-grain rice
7 fl oz/225 ml/scant 1 cup
   chicken stock
1 lb 12 oz/800 g canned
   chopped tomatoes
1 tbsp chopped fresh thyme
2 tbsp chopped fresh oregano
12 black olives, pitted and chopped
2 oz/55 g Feta cheese, crumbled
fresh oregano sprigs, to garnish

method

1 Remove the skin from the chicken. Heat the oil in a flameproof casserole. Add the chicken, in batches, if necessary, and cook over medium heat, turning occasionally, for 8–10 minutes, or until golden. Transfer to a plate with a perforated spoon.

2 Add the onion, garlic, long-grain rice, and 2 fl oz/50 ml/scant ¼ cup of the stock to the casserole and cook, stirring, for 5 minutes, or until the onion is softened. Pour in the remaining stock and add the tomatoes and their juices and the herbs.

3 Return the chicken thighs to the casserole, pushing them down into the rice. Bring to a boil, then reduce the heat, cover, and simmer for 25–30 minutes, or until the chicken is cooked through and tender. Stir in the olives and sprinkle the cheese on top. Garnish with oregano sprigs and serve immediately.

jambalaya

ingredients

serves 4

14 oz/400 g skinless, boneless
    chicken breast, diced

1 red onion, diced

1 garlic clove, crushed

20 fl oz/625 ml/2½ cups
    chicken stock

14 oz/400 g canned chopped
    tomatoes in tomato juice

10 oz/280 g/generous 1½ cups
    brown rice

1–2 tsp hot chili powder

½ tsp paprika

1 tsp dried oregano

1 red bell pepper, seeded
    and diced

1 yellow bell pepper, seeded
    and diced

3 oz/85 g/½ cup frozen corn kernels

3 oz/85 g/½ cup frozen peas

3 tbsp chopped fresh parsley

pepper

crisp salad greens, to serve

method

1 Put the chicken, onion, garlic, stock, tomatoes, and rice into a large, heavy-bottom pan. Add the chili powder, paprika, and oregano and stir well. Bring to a boil, then reduce the heat, cover, and let simmer for 25 minutes.

2 Add the red and yellow bell peppers, corn, and peas to the rice mixture and return to a boil. Reduce the heat, cover, and let simmer for an additional 10 minutes, or until the rice is just tender (brown rice retains a 'nutty' texture when cooked) and most of the stock has been absorbed but is not completely dry.

3 Stir in 2 tablespoons of the parsley and season with pepper. Transfer the jambalaya to a warmed serving dish, garnish with the remaining parsley, and serve with crisp salad greens.

egg-fried rice with chicken

ingredients

serves 4

8 oz/225 g/generous 1 cup jasmine rice

3 skinless, boneless chicken breasts, cut into cubes

14 fl oz/400 ml/1¾ cups canned coconut milk

1¾ oz/50 g block creamed coconut, chopped

2–3 cilantro roots, chopped

thinly pared zest of 1 lemon

1 fresh green chile, seeded and chopped

3 fresh Thai basil leaves

1 tbsp fish sauce

1 tbsp oil

3 eggs, beaten

fresh chives and sprigs fresh cilantro, to garnish

method

1 Cook the rice in boiling water for 12–15 minutes, drain well, then let cool and chill overnight.

2 Put the chicken into a pan and cover with the coconut milk. Add the creamed coconut, cilantro roots, lemon zest, and chile, and bring to a boil. Let simmer for 8–10 minutes, until the chicken is tender. Remove from the heat. Stir in the basil and fish sauce.

3 Meanwhile, heat the oil in a wok and stir-fry the rice for 2–3 minutes. Pour in the eggs and stir until they have cooked and mixed with the rice. Line 4 small ovenproof bowls or ramekins with plastic wrap and pack with the rice. Turn out carefully onto serving plates and remove the plastic wrap. Garnish with long chives and sprigs of cilantro. Serve with the chicken.

hainan chicken rice

ingredients

serves 4–6

1 chicken, weighing
    3 lb 5 oz/1.5 kg
2 oz/55 g fresh young ginger,
    smashed
2 garlic cloves, smashed
1 scallion, tied in a knot
1 tsp salt
2 tbsp vegetable or peanut oil
chili or soy dipping sauce,
    to serve

rice

2 tbsp vegetable or peanut oil
5 garlic cloves, finely chopped
5 shallots, finely chopped
12 oz/350 g/scant 1¾ cups
    long-grain rice
30 fl oz/940 ml/3¾ cups
    chicken stock
1 tsp salt

method

1 Wash the chicken and dry thoroughly. Stuff the body cavity with the ginger, garlic, scallion, and salt.

2 In a large pan, bring enough water to a boil to submerge the chicken. Place the chicken in the pan, breast-side down. Bring the water back to a boil, then turn down the heat and simmer, covered, for 30–40 minutes. Turn the chicken over once.

3 Remove the chicken and wash in running cold water for 2 minutes to stop the cooking. Drain, then rub the oil into the skin. Set aside.

4 To prepare the rice, heat the oil in a preheated wok or deep pan. Stir-fry the garlic and shallots until fragrant. Add the rice and cook for 3 minutes, stirring rapidly. Transfer to a large pan and add the chicken stock and salt. Bring to a boil, then turn down the heat and let simmer, covered, for 20 minutes. Turn off the heat and let steam for an additional 5–10 minutes, or until the rice is perfectly cooked.

5 To serve, chop the chicken horizontally through the bone and skin into chunky wedges. Serve with the rice and a chili or soy dipping sauce.

chicken steamed with rice in lotus leaves

ingredients

serves 4–8

1 lb/450 g/generous 2 cups glutinous rice, soaked in cold water for 2 hours

16 fl oz/450 ml/1¾ cups cold water

1 tsp salt

1 tsp vegetable or peanut oil

4 dried lotus leaves, soaked in hot water for 1 hour

filling

3½ oz/100 g raw small shrimp, shelled and deveined

2-inch/5-cm piece fresh ginger

7 oz/200 g lean chicken meat, cut into bite-size strips

2 tsp light soy sauce

2 oz/55 g dried Chinese mushrooms, soaked in warm water for 20 minutes

1 tbsp vegetable or peanut oil

7 oz/200 g cha siu or pork loin

1 tbsp Shaoxing rice wine

1 tsp dark soy sauce

½ tsp white pepper

1 tsp sugar

method

1 For the filling, steam the shrimp for 5 minutes and set aside. Finely grate the ginger, discarding the fibrous parts on the grater and reserving the liquid that drips through. Marinate the chicken in the light soy sauce and ginger juices for at least 20 minutes. Steam for a few minutes in the marinade. Set aside.

2 Drain the rice and place in a pan with the water. Bring to a boil, then add the salt and oil. Cover and cook over very low heat for 15 minutes. Divide into 8 portions and set aside. Squeeze out any excess water from the mushrooms, then finely slice, discarding any tough stems. Reserve the soaking water. In a preheated wok or deep pan, heat the oil and stir-fry the pork, shrimp, and mushrooms for 2 minutes. Stir in the Shaoxing, dark soy sauce, pepper, and sugar. Add the reserved mushroom soaking water, if necessary.

3 Rinse and dry the lotus leaves. Place a portion of rice in the center of each and flatten out to form a 4-inch/10-cm square. Top with the pork mixture and some pieces of chicken. Top with another portion of rice, then fold the lotus leaf to form a tight package. Steam for about 15 minutes. Let rest for 5 minutes, then serve.

chicken with vegetables & cilantro rice

ingredients

serves 4

2 tbsp vegetable or peanut oil

1 red onion, chopped

2 garlic cloves, chopped

1-inch/2.5-cm piece fresh ginger, peeled and chopped

2 skinless, boneless chicken breasts, cut into strips

4 oz/115 g white mushrooms

14 oz/400 g canned coconut milk

2 oz/50 g sugar snap peas, trimmed and halved lengthwise

2 tbsp soy sauce

1 tbsp fish sauce

rice

1 tbsp vegetable or peanut oil

1 red onion, sliced

12 oz/350 g/3 cups rice, cooked and cooled

8 oz/250 g bok choy, torn into large pieces

handful of fresh cilantro, chopped

2 tbsp Thai soy sauce

method

1 Heat the oil in a wok or large skillet and sauté the onion, garlic, and ginger together for 1–2 minutes.

2 Add the chicken and mushrooms and cook over high heat until browned. Add the coconut milk, sugar snap peas, and sauces, and bring to a boil. Let simmer gently for 4–5 minutes until tender.

3 Heat the oil for the rice in a separate wok or large skillet and cook the onion until softened, but not browned. Add the cooked rice, bok choy, and fresh cilantro, and heat gently until the leaves have wilted and the rice is hot. Sprinkle over the soy sauce and serve immediately with the chicken.

chicken biryani

ingredients

serves 8

1½ tsp finely chopped fresh ginger

1½ tsp crushed fresh garlic

1 tbsp garam masala

1 tsp chili powder

½ tsp ground turmeric

2 tsp salt

5 green/white cardamom
   pods, crushed

10 fl oz/300 ml/1¼ cups
   plain yogurt

3 lb 5 oz/1.5 kg chicken, skinned
   and cut into 8 parts

5 fl oz/150 ml/⅔ cup milk

1 tsp saffron strands

6 tbsp ghee

2 onions, sliced

1 lb/450 g basmati rice

2 cinnamon sticks

4 black peppercorns

1 tsp black cumin seeds

4 fresh green chiles

4 tbsp lemon juice

2–3 tbsp finely chopped fresh
   cilantro leaves

method

1 Blend the ginger, garlic, garam masala, chili powder, turmeric, half the salt, and the cardamoms together in a bowl. Add the yogurt and chicken parts and mix well. Cover and let marinate in the refrigerator for 3 hours.

2 Boil the milk in a small pan, pour over the saffron, and set aside.

3 Heat the ghee in a large pan. Add the onions and cook until golden. Transfer half of the onions and ghee to a bowl and set aside.

4 Place the rice, cinnamon sticks, peppercorns, and black cumin seeds in a pan of water. Bring to a boil and remove from the heat when the rice is half-cooked. Drain and place in a bowl. Mix with the remaining salt.

5 Chop the chiles and set aside. Add the chicken mixture to the pan containing the onions. Add half each of the chopped green chiles, lemon juice, cilantro, and saffron milk. Add the rice, then the rest of the ingredients, including the reserved onions and ghee. Cover tightly and cook over low heat for 1 hour. Check that the meat is cooked through; if it is not cooked, return to the heat, and cook for an additional 15 minutes. Mix well before serving.

index